The Institute of Religion
Series on Religion and Health Care #2

Testing the Medical Covenant

Active Euthanasia and Health Care Reform

WILLIAM F. MAY

WILLIAM B. EERDMANS PUBLISHING COMPANY
GRAND RAPIDS, MICHIGAN / CAMBRIDGE, U.K.

© 1996 Wm. B. Eerdmans Publishing Co.
255 Jefferson Ave. S.E., Grand Rapids, Michigan 49503 /
P.O. Box 163, Cambridge CB3 9PU U.K.

Printed in the United States of America

01 00 99 98 97 96   7 6 5 4 3 2 1

Library of Congress Cataloging-in-Publication Data

May, William F.
Testing the medical covenant: active euthanasia
and health care reform / William F. May
p.   cm.
Includes index.
ISBN 0-8028-4204-6 (alk. paper)
1. Medical ethics. 2. Euthanasia — Moral and ethical aspects.
3. Health care reform — Moral and ethical aspects. I. Title.
R724.M286 1996
174'.2 — dc20   96-26076
                                  CIP

A covenant exists . . . between all the citizens of a democracy when they all feel themselves subject to the same weakness and the same dangers; their interests as well as their compassion makes it a rule with them to lend one another assistance when required.

ALEXIS DE TOCQUEVILLE

The Institute of Religion
Series on Religion and Health Care

The Institute of Religion was founded in 1954 by some visionaries in the Texas Medical Center who saw the importance of nurturing a conversation between medicine and religion. It was first a trailblazer in the training for hospital chaplaincy and then a trailblazer in the conversations that became the field of medical ethics.

The Institute of Religion continues to support research, education, and service at the intersection of health care and religious commitment. Books in this series are the result of theological reflection at that intersection. They are offered as a service to those in health care who want to understand and undertake their work as a calling, as a form of ministry to the sick. They are offered as a service to those in the academy who would attend — and have their students attend — to the voices of faith seeking understanding of human suffering and the responses of health care. And they are offered as a service to members of believing communities who would support, encourage, and admonish one another, including those in their midst who are sick, suffering, or dying and those in their midst with the vocation to care for the sick, suffering, or dying.

For
my daughters
Catherine and Elisabeth

Contents

Acknowledgments

Like most writers in the field of medical ethics, I have benefited from invitations to give lectures and papers before various inter-professional groups. These invitations to present and publish in various stages and settings provide the teacher with the inspiration of broader audiences, the psychological necessity of deadlines, and the opportunity to weather some criticism and self-criticism before developing the final versions of the chapters in a book controlled by his or her own overriding theme.

The questions posed by this book grow naturally out of my earlier work on *The Physician's Covenant* and *The Patient's Ordeal.* What is the reach of the medical covenant — particularly as it touches upon the ordeal of the dying patient? What should be the scope of the medical covenant — as it covers or fails to cover all citizens? What virtues should we look for in the covenanted physician and nurse? Under the pressure of these questions, the chapters have undergone a series of growth rings beyond their original planting. Sometimes the final result hardly resembles the original. Still, I must acknowledge — and gratefully — the opportunity to work out earlier, shorter drafts of material for each of the chapters. They include the following:

"Moral and Religious Reservations about Euthanasia," in *Must We Suffer Our Way to Death?* (Dallas: Southern Methodist University Press, 1966).

"The Virtues in a Professional Setting," in *Medicine and Moral Reasoning,* ed. K. W. M. Fulford, Grant Gillett, and Janet Martin Soskice (Cambridge: Cambridge University Press, 1994), pp. 75-90.

"The Medical Covenant: An Ethics of Obligation or Virtue?" in *Theological Analyses of the Clinical Encounter,* ed. Gerald P. McKenny and Jonathan R. Sande (Norwell, Mass.: Kluwer Academic Publishers, 1994), pp. 29-44.

"The Ethics of Health Care Reform," in *The Annual of the Society of Christian Ethics* (Washington: Georgetown University Press, 1994), pp. 171-86.

Ann and Cary M. Maguire of Dallas endowed the chair I hold at Southern Methodist University. Their generous support has given me the privilege of writing and teaching since 1985.

My thanks also go to Dr. Allen D. Verhey, former director of the Institute of Religion at the Texas Medical Center in Houston, who invited me to give a series of lectures there linking the subject of active euthanasia with the virtues required in professional life. That proposal and invitation evolved into this book, which editors Jon Pott and Tim Straayer of the William B. Eerdmans Publishing Company have kindly steered toward its publication.

Once again, I am grateful beyond payback to A. Lewis Soens of the University of Notre Dame for his vigorous reading of the chapters. He pushes authors toward more precision and detail than they would ordinarily attain. However, blame the private, not the drill sergeant, for whatever imprecision still remains. Professor Soens's friendship since 1954 has given me one of the grace notes of my professional life.

Ms. Carol Swartz has served as my administrative assistant

throughout the writing of this book and prepared more versions of the text than either she surely cares to, or the computer can, remember. Her good humor, friendship, courtesy, and skill place me permanently in her debt.

I have dedicated this book to my daughters, Catherine and Elisabeth, both physicians, wives, and mothers who have learned beautifully and bravely how to fulfill each role — distinctively on their own, to be sure, but with fine models as well in their mother and each other.

Introduction

In the course of the fall of 1994, two events tested the nature of the medical covenant in the United States. The voters in Oregon approved narrowly by ballot initiative (51% to 49%) Measure 16, which would, for the first time in one of the states, allow doctors to prescribe lethal drugs for the specific purpose of ending a patient's life; and the U.S. Congress not merely rejected but resoundingly refused even to pass out of committee any of the bills that would have reformed the national health care system.

The near simultaneous success of the euthanasia measure and the failure to reform the national health care system may not be entirely coincidental. The same libertarian spirit that led to change in Oregon ("I should be totally free to choose how I die") may have also contributed to the fear of any change in the health care system emanating from Washington, D.C. ("I should be totally free to choose my doctor" and "Doctors should be totally free to practice without interference from Washington").

The debate over active euthanasia tests the national medical covenant. Does the traditional medical covenant go far enough in assisting patients? Has the doctor or the nurse refused to go the final mile with the patient in declining to euthanize or assist in his or her suicide? What do professionals owe patients when their remedies

1

no longer cure, when their drugs fail to lighten pain, and when a suffering patient asks for relief through death? Do healers at the last moment break their covenant with the patient when they refuse to administer or to assist in administering the sodium pentathol, carbon monoxide, or the just-in-case plastic bag that secures peace at the last for the beleaguered patient? And if some health care professionals are ready to push their services to the limit by ushering patients into the grave, does society harm the patient by prohibiting the professional from giving this last professional service? Has the society broken the covenant that Tocqueville said exists between all the citizens of a democracy? Have citizens failed in the compassion that "makes it a rule with them to lend one another assistance when required"?

Answers to these questions about the professional and the society's covenant with the dying depend, in part, on an answer to a second question. Does the professional profess a body of knowledge directed solely to fighting against death or to eliminating suffering? If only the fight against death justifies the professional, then the professional can only fight to preserve life. So viewed, the professional must refrain from practicing not only active but passive euthanasia, not only mercy killing but allowing to die.

If, on the other hand, the relief of suffering, not the fight against death, is the end of medicine, physicians (and the society through them) fail their art and the patient if they stand by while the patient suffers, if they fail to eliminate that suffering, even, if need be, by killing.

Still others argue that neither fighting death nor relieving suffering is the final goal of medicine. Each contributes to that goal, but each is secondary to it. *Health* is the ultimate end of medicine; *healing* is its art. Usually the physician fights death. Certainly she must fight when she can restore the patient to health, but when the fight against death only prolongs dying, it is better to let the dying patient die. Letting the patient die, they argue, is not itself devoid of healing if healing in the old sense of "making whole" takes place in the midst of the patient's dying. This perspective argues for a medical covenant with the dying that neither an unconditional fight against death nor mercy killing adequately defines.

Usually, the doctor relieves pain and suffering. But not invariably. Sometimes the physician must impose pain in order to heal; and sometimes caregivers must suffer with sufferers rather than try to eliminate a pain that only worsens with the effort to banish it altogether. (For example, the overdose of an antidepressant eliminated an older cancer patient's perception of pain, but it also threw him into a psychotic state that deprived him of his senses and deprived his wife of her husband. The doctor wisely withdrew to more modest efforts to reduce his pain.)

From this perspective, the fights against death and suffering are secondary to the pursuit of health. Leon Kass defined health as the well-working of the organism as a whole.[1] Physicians and other healers assist in making and keeping patients whole, so far as possible, in the course of their living and dying. The hospice movement has particularly emphasized the need for such healing in the midst of dying.

The two extremes of an unconditional fight against death and an unlimited effort to eliminate suffering, while opposed as ends, resemble one another in their perception of the healer. They both see the healer as a contractor of services directed specifically and exclusively to one or the other of these ends. The healer sells technical means to combat or control death in the one instance and suffering in the other. A contract, in general, is limited and time-bound — whether a contract to build a house, to fix plumbing, or, in this instance, to aim the guns of medicine against one or the other of these two evils.

Commercial contracts demand only what the contract specifies,

1. Kass, *Toward a More Natural Science* (New York: Free Press, 1985), p. 174.

and they do not transform any of the parties involved. In contrast, a covenant, such as the covenants of religious people before God or the covenants of friendship and marriage, engages and transforms the inner identity of both parties involved in it. A healer's covenant fully commits the practitioner; it does not simply fragment time and action into billable hours and procedures. It also requires the healer to attend to the patient as a whole rather than to treat the patient's case as a skirmish in a generalized war against either death or suffering. Much medical service, perforce, takes place contractually, since people often require specific, limited services. But somewhere in health care, in addition to the all-monitoring eye of cardiac equipment, CAT scans, and magnetic resonance imaging (and the maneuvers that they dictate), the covenanted healer must be attentive to the whole patient and assist in keeping and honoring her as a whole in the course of her living and dying.

The national debate over the reform of the health care system provided the second major test of the medical covenant in 1994. The debate in the nineties over health care reform erupted on the national scene with the unexpected election of an uncharismatic former college president, Harris Wofford of Pennsylvania, to complete an unexpired two-year term in the U.S. Senate. Wofford made reforming health care the decisive issue in his campaign. His victory, as the Democratic candidate, signaled, at least for the moment, an intense public interest in health care reform. But the interest and pressure receded rapidly during the following two years. In the November 1994 election, Senator Wofford failed to win a full six-year term, and the Republican party won, for the first time in fifty years, control of both houses of Congress without so much as a mention of national health care reform in its much-publicized Contract with America.

The proponents of reform believed that the medical covenant between America and its citizens is a sham as long as almost a third of the nation is either uninsured or underinsured. Whether by taxes or by some combination of taxes and employer-mandated insurance, the advocates of reform have argued, our nation must find ways to meet the medical and health care needs of its citizens. Maintaining its citizens' health ought, at least, to match the national commitment to maintaining highways, factories, and machines. If the government rightly orders its priorities, caring for its citizens' health will simply be part of the cost of doing the nation's business.

The debate about health care reform, like that about active euthanasia, goes to the core of the medical covenant. It tests the covenant's scope — both its universality and its comprehensiveness.

Who is the someone on behalf of whom the professional (and the society through the professional) professes the art of healing? Who is the patient? Only those affluent enough to pay for their treatment but not those too poor to pay? Those able to rouse my charitable impulse but not those whose dependence irritates me? People with jobs that provide third-party coverage but not the working poor who struggle on minimum wage without fringe benefits? The elderly covered by Medicare but not the unemployed under sixty-five who lose health care coverage when they lose a job? Should not the medical covenant offer universal access to our fellow citizens?

The debate over health care reform poses still further questions about the comprehensiveness of the medical covenant. Does health care chug along in the Intensive Care Unit but then stall when the patient reaches home? Does it treat the patient with physical ailments but overlook the person tortured mentally? Does it offer a rich menu of nostrums but respond with stony silence to those hypochondriacs whose habits drive them from palliative to palliative? Does it ingeniously drag out dying without offering relief or consolation to the dying? Does the system pour research money into the fight against death at the expense of looking into how we might help patients die more peacefully? Some of these questions suggest that the discrete policy issues of passive and active euthanasia cannot be satisfactorily resolved without some reflection on the scope of the medical covenant — its comprehensiveness and its universality. If health care fails to reach everybody and to offer the kinds of services the dying need, just how voluntary is voluntary euthanasia, just how compassionate is mercy killing?

Those opposed to universal and comprehensive health care shifted political discussion in the mid-nineties largely to issues of budget deficits and tax cuts. Their health care reform proposal chiefly amounted to reducing the cost of Medicare and Medicaid by some $270 billion so as to accommodate a faster reduction in the budget deficit (by $30 billion) and to cut taxes (by $230 billion). This conservative agenda does not wholly ignore the question of covenantal obligation. Health care is, after all, only one of a series of goods and services to which the nation is committed. And cost is a significant consideration in many moral issues. Even those who oppose the conservative agenda and back comprehensive health care reform have cited the need to control costs as one of their arguments for more ambitious reform of the system. However, they do not believe that reducing Medicare costs alone will control rising health care costs or aid in reaching universal and comprehensive coverage.

Both major parties to the debate have edged toward covenantal language to back their positions. Clinton, a Baptist president, invoked the scriptural term *covenant* when he spoke of a "new covenant" in his 1993 inaugural address. Whatever his motive, he used a term relevant to the politics of the nation. The Republicans mobilized their electoral rebuttal by appealing to the term *contract* when they offered their Contract with America. Thus the debate has been joined.

I shall not attempt to decipher the Democratic and Republican meanings for the terms *covenant* and *contract*. In my own use of the word *contract*, I mean simply commercial transactions between buyers and sellers. People usually have such commercial exchanges in mind when they seek to solve the problem of health care reform by appealing to market forces. A commercial contract presupposes, in general, two relatively informed parties, each guided by self-interest, who enter into an agreement to exchange money for goods and services. The contract specifies and delimits the goods and services offered for a particular price, and payment obliges the seller to deliver those services but no more. Professionals, as distinct from amateurs, participate in the marketplace. Physicians receive either a fee for service, a salary from an organization, or a financial return from a "capitation" system (in which physicians profit from the difference between an annual payment per person or family and the cost of services rendered).

A contractualist understanding of professional responsibility has obvious appeal. It breaks with more authoritarian, parentalist models of professional power over patients; it seems to place the patient on equal terms with the doctor and the hospital as buyer with seller; and it promotes standards of informed, uncoerced, and self-interested consent. Moreover, the explicit details of a contract offer a basis for the legal enforcement of its terms, thus providing some protection for both parties.

Despite these advantages, however, a mercantile, contractualist ethic does not fully satisfy the requirements either for a professional ethic or for a health care delivery system. Since self-interest guides both parties in a commercial transaction, and since the seller, particularly in a professional relationship, enjoys a huge edge over the buyer in expertise, an old warning hangs over the gate to the marketplace: "Let the buyer beware." A purely contractualist understanding of the professional relationship has produced professionals too driven by their own self-interest and, depending on incentives, tempts them either to undertreat or to overtreat their patients.

In general, a contractual fee-for-service system (in which a third party pays the fees) has tempted professionals and hospitals to overtreat patients. The more treatment and the more time spent in the hospital, the more money physicians and hospitals make. (The practice of "defensive medicine" — to ward off malpractice suits —

has compounded the problem of overtreatment and the rising cost of health care.) Conversely, the increasingly popular yearly payment system, in which physicians and hospitals profit from minimizing their costs, encourages undertreatment. Runaway self-interest provides the link between the apparently contradictory strategies of too much and too little. It fueled the skyrocketing costs of fee-for-service medicine, which has in turn led reactively to the sometimes stultifying controls and grudging service of managed care. The current system also leaves too many without care or without the right kinds of care. The national covenant to assist one another of which Tocqueville wrote has diminished into a contract.

The concept of a covenant provides a more spacious framework for interpreting the professional's full obligation to a patient and the nation's needs in a health care system. Covenants and contracts resemble one another: both depend upon a promise and an exchange.[2] A contract governs buying and selling on the basis of each party's self-interest. This is why one must read a contract warily. But a covenant — for example, the covenant of marriage or friendship — includes the additional elements of disinterested giving and receiving that may carry the parties beyond the partial and limited terms of a contract. A contract specifies, limits, and restricts, requiring only what it enjoins. A covenant more deeply engages both parties. The letter of a contract establishes its territorial limits; the spirit of a covenant often carries those covenanted together beyond the letter of the law into the domain of the unexpected.

The professional exchange surely includes a contractualist element. Professionals receive money for their work, and a society must pay, either through taxes or through some other device, for its health care system. But the professional exchange, as covenanted, must also

---

2. For a more extended discussion of the contrast between a contract and a covenant, see William F. May, *The Physician's Covenant* (Louisville: Westminster/John Knox Press, 1983), pp. 116-30 and chap. 6.

transcend the marketplace transaction of buying and selling. The professional professes something (the art of healing) on behalf of someone (the patient). This double fidelity to the art of healing and to the patient generates trust. This is why we call the professional relationship *fiduciary.* For healing to work, the patient must assume that the professional will not merely treat him as a profit opportunity, and the professional perforce builds safeguards into the system. But something else besides a piece of paper must hold self-interest in check and let the disinterested work of healing take place. The name for this additional ingredient of good faith that binds persons and communities together is *covenant.*

Unavoidably, the nation will face a third test of the medical covenant. The issues of active euthanasia and health care reform have dominated the public debate in the nineties because they directly test the society's commitment to health care. But a society, in good part, fulfills that commitment through its health care professionals. Thus the social issues cannot be fully explored without considering the requisite character and virtues of those who must make good on policies governing the end of life and must supply health care within the limits of a very complex system, whether reformed or not. Patients cannot adequately protect themselves. They usually do not have enough knowledge to follow the marketplace advice to be wary of the physician, or of the hospital, or of the health care plan. Medical crisis sometimes does not give them time for comparative shopping, and the unpredictable contingencies of illness do not permit a detailed contractual specification of all services required. Healers must be ready to cope in good faith with the contingent and the unexpected. Calls upon services may exceed those specified in a contract or the compensation available in a given case. But even if one could supply patients with the knowledge they needed to be sufficiently wary, suspicion hardly provides the best environment for effective healing. Neither can any policy or system, however ingeniously devised, fully protect citizens and patients against mediocre or vicious performance. The success of policies and reforms depends, at least in part, upon the virtue of the major players charged with executing those policies and with performing well despite the stress of changes in the system.

Character and virtue generally arise in the midst of difficulty and adversity. The virtues enable us, in the words of the philosopher Alasdair MacIntyre, "to overcome the various particular harms, dangers, temptations and distractions which we encounter in attempting to sustain those goods internal to practices" such as medicine, nursing, and healing.[3] Adversity looms large in sustaining the goods internal to the work of health care practitioners because they must face into the ordeals of those to whom they give care. Professionals bring to these arduous tasks some gifts of intellect and temperament. But these natural gifts differ from character and virtue. Nature imposes our temperament: it deals us our cards, some good, some inconvenient. But we choose how we play the hand. (We cannot, of course, claim sole credit for our character and virtue. The examples others set for us, the money, time, and care they have invested in defining us as citizens, spouses, and professionals, and the grace note of the support they have given us when we did not deserve it should prevent us from preening in the conceit that we are self-made men and women).

In addition to the public tests to which the issues of euthanasia and health care reform subject the nation, physicians and other healers today must pass their own personal tests as they face into the ordeals of their patients and the stresses of the institutions in which they work. The particular virtues professionals require are not unique to them. Professionals are not a subspecies of human beings on a reservation of their own. They need some of the same virtues as other humans — but, most specifically, prudence, fidelity, and

3. MacIntyre, *After Virtue: A Study in Moral Theory* (Notre Dame, Ind.: University of Notre Dame Press, 1981), p. 204.

public-spiritedness. These three virtues correlate closely with the several characteristics — intellectual, moral, and organizational — that we customarily and reasonably associate with a professional's identity. Intellectually, the professional requires prudence (that is, attentiveness and discernment); morally, fidelity; and organizationally, public-spiritedness.

If the end of medicine were simply a generalized fight against death or the elimination of suffering, physicians would not particularly need the virtue of prudence; they could simply apply their scientific knowledge and skill to the case of the bone cancer victim in Room 407, for example. If, however, the ultimate end of medicine is healing, in the sense of making the patient whole in the midst of her living and dying, then that task calls for the play of the virtue of prudence. It calls for a disciplined attentiveness to the patient as a whole. It calls for a careful discernment of what distinguishes the patient's case from those of others and what services are called for. Prudence, if you will, serves as the eyes and ears of the covenant with the patient. It allows the healer to stay with the patient, even in her dying. The attentiveness of prudence helps protect "allowing to die" from sliding into abandonment.

Fidelity embodies charity in health care — charity here meaning not the sentiment of love but a resolution of the will that impels the professional and the nation beyond the quid pro quos of buying and selling toward the more inclusive goal of disinterested giving. The covenanted health care system needs to be spacious enough to reach all citizens and attend to their healing in their dying as well as their living.

The third virtue of public-spiritedness was relatively untested during the period when most physicians practiced solo. But public-spiritedness, understood as the art of acting in concert with others for the common good, grows in importance today. Physicians are increasingly responsible for producing health care services in the complex social settings of the hospital, the clinic, and the health care team. They must increasingly accept responsibility for controlling the quality of those services, thereby involving themselves in the vexing issues of self-regulation and discipline; and, as the wielders of significant power, they must participate in the debate over the fair distribution of health care resources. The current aggravation over institutional change — however justified or unjustified it may be — places a particularly heavy demand on this virtue today.

Finally, if we let the word *covenant* carry us back to its religious source, we will be more inclined to see the deeper setting and test for these generally recognizable virtues in the virtues of gratitude and hope.

Does the Medical Covenant Require the Practice of Active Euthanasia and Assistance in Suicide?

Movements in Western medical ethics today usually divide into two camps — the pro-lifers and the pro-quality-of-lifers. The pro-lifers tend to see death as the absolute evil; the quality-of-lifers, suffering.

I cannot join either camp. I have been shaped by the biblical tradition, and my reluctance springs from theological grounds. The theistic tradition recognizes neither *life* nor *wealth of life* as an absolute good; they are fundamental goods, derived from God, but not themselves divine. Further, neither death nor suffering is an absolute evil; neither can deprive human beings of that which is absolutely good. The goods and ills we know in life are finally creaturely and relative. We are free to enjoy goods but not to worship them. We can regret their loss but must not despair. We are charged to resist evil but must not assume that this resistance alone provides our final meaning and resource.

This theologically developed position does not inevitably establish in ethics a distinctive or unique set of guidelines. It does not always call for a distinctive action, but it does somewhat brighten the sky under which we act — it clears the sky of the despair those suffer

13

who believe that except for life, there is only death or that except for a rich quality-of-life, there is only the final impoverishment of the soul.

We need not view the moral life as a grim struggle of life against death or of quality-of-life against poverty. Neither should our political life disintegrate into a fierce conflict between pro-lifers and the pro-quality-of-lifers, each heaping epithets on the other, each charging the other with moral blindness. Both absolutistic positions are ultimately too shrill to control their advocates' own excesses: one group clamors in panic for life at all cost; the other shouts "Give me quality-of-life or give me (or them) death."

A more relaxed theological perspective suggests that decisions should vary in different cases: sometimes to relieve suffering, at other times to resist death. But in any event, decisions should not spring from that fear and despair which often creates the absolutist in ethics. (Of course, others than theists can hold to this perspective on ethics. A variety of other religious and secular positions might also criticize the absolutist commitments of the pro-lifers and the pro-quality-of-lifers. I have simply attempted to acknowledge the theological source of my own reservations about the two movements.)

In the debates over public policy, a theist ought not, in my judgment, to side with either camp in its extreme form. The first group would define the medical profession wholly by a contract to fight against death. I believe that the physician's covenant should free physicians to respond to patients' requests to cease and desist in the effort to prolong dying when treatment can no longer serve the health of the host. Maximal treatment is not always optimal care. Sometimes concern for health makes it sensible not only to withhold but to withdraw treatment. A physician does not always have the duty to fight pneumonia if the patient prefers such death to imminent death by irreversible cancer. There is, after all, a time to live and a time to die and a fitting time for allowing to die, the name for which is *passive euthanasia.*

At the same time, I do not think it wise for a society to adopt as a general public policy the opposite extreme. Neither physicians nor the society at large ought to prize the quality of life so highly that they seek to solve the problem of suffering by eliminating the sufferer. This is the solution to evil offered by the advocates of active euthanasia. It aims to relieve suffering by knocking out the interval between life and death, to make one dead as quickly as possible.

The impulse behind the movement for active euthanasia is understandable in an age when dying has become such a protracted, inhumanly endless business at the hands of people committed to fight death at any price. But active euthanasia goes beyond the middle course of the right to die and insists upon the right to be killed and therefore the duty or privilege to kill. It solves the problem of a runaway *technical* medicine by resorting, finally, to *technique*. It opposes the horrors of a purely technically extended death by using technique to eliminate the victim. It insufficiently honors the human capacity to cope with life once terminal pain and suffering have appeared. It fears that humanity cannot suffuse dying as well as living.

In general, I think a physician's covenant can allow the terminal patient (who requests it) to die, but I have serious reservations about policies that regularize mercy killing.

On Drawing Lines

Some people would argue that the distinction between allowing to die and mercy killing is hypocritical quibbling over technique. They would collapse the distinction between passive and active euthanasia. Since the patient dies — whether by acts of merciful omission or commission — what matters the route the patient took to get there? By either procedure he ends up dead. Since modern procedures, moreover, have made dying at the hands of the experts and their machines a prolonged and painful business, why not move beyond the right to die to the right to be killed?

John Fletcher, an ethicist at the University of Virginia, has called the distinction between active and passive euthanasia a "worn-out" distinction, or, if not worn-out, arbitrary and misleading. We have kept to the distinction partly because fatal *actions* appear worse than fatal *omissions*. But everyone can think of exceptions to that appearance. Some actions that lead to death are acceptable. For example, one may justifiably administer large doses of morphine to relieve severe pain, even though the morphine may also, as an anticipated but unintended second effect, hasten the patient's death.[1] Meanwhile some omissions that lead to death are reprehensible. For example, deliberately failing to treat an ordinary patient's bacterial pneumonia when she could recover and live productively and ignoring a bleeding patient's pleas for help are very serious wrongs. The moral justification in each case depends upon the motive and intent of the agent and the wishes of the patient rather than on the act defined as an omission or a commission.

However, the fact that exceptional cases cross the boundary that generally distinguishes one practice from another does not of itself argue against respecting a line between the two practices. First and stipulatively, a society often needs to draw a line between two practices despite the embarrassment of exceptional cases that cross the boundary between them. A particular fifteen-year-old adolescent may be more mature than the average seventeen-year-old, but that does not of itself invalidate a line somewhere, usually sixteen, specifying an age requirement for a driver's license. On a given piece of land, one may not see a line over which one steps from the U.S.A. into Canada or from Arizona into Mexico; nevertheless, reasons may

---

1. The carefully constructed Roman Catholic doctrine of "double effect" would not justify administering an overdose of morphine with the intention of killing the patient.

exist for drawing territorial boundary lines, even in the absence of such obvious geographical markers as a lake, an ocean, a river, a mountain range, or a fence. Upon such fine (or unseen) lines civilized life often depends.

Second and substantively, nature has already drawn a line between a death that nature brings about — if we only let it — and a death that we wreak on ourselves or others. This substantial distinction between natural and human agency supplies a much weightier reason for respecting the distinction between passive and active euthanasia than the general need to draw a line somewhere. However, our modern ambition to conquer nature has tended to render nature invisible to us. Increasingly, we focus only on human motive and intent, and nature slips from view. Scrutinizing motives surely helps us examine and assess a particular person and his act, but it also has the effect of systematically banishing from view the important boundary underlying the traditional prohibition against active euthanasia and the acceptance of passive euthanasia — the boundary between natural and human agency. In allowing to die, the physician, the nurse, and the family simply step out of the way to let a host of natural forces aggressively bring a life to its end. In active euthanasia and in assisted suicide, a human being does the killing. We ought not to conflate the two. The human motive may be compassion in both cases, but there remains a difference between letting the patient die and killing the patient. The conflation of letting die and killing banishes nature from view and reduces all events to options under human control. When we scrutinize a particular act, we may well need to focus on the human agent; the motives of malice and pity obviously differ. But when it comes to ordering human society and practices and drawing the lines between practices on which civilized life depends, we cannot casually ignore the great boundary between nature and the human. That boundary surpasses all those intramural boundaries within nature upon which we seize to draw our maps — mountains, rivers, lakes, oceans, and stars. At the least, we should make sure that our reasons for crossing the border are weighty and not merely routine.

The Arguments in Favor

Two of the five major arguments for active euthanasia surface in the very terms "voluntary euthanasia" and "mercy killing." First, active euthanasianists believe that respect for the patient's autonomy should finally govern care for the dying. If we legally prohibit active euthanasia, we fail to respect the liberty of those who want the doctor's assistance in ending their dying. It's a free country, and freedom ought to extend to the choice of one's final exit. The patient who consents to his being killed or asks assistance in suicide presumably harms no other person. Thus, a legal prohibition against assisted suicide or euthanasia seems unjustified and arbitrary.

Second, active euthanasianists appeal to the compassion of the caregiver with the term "mercy killing." If we do not have the option of active euthanasia, they argue, we cannot act as compassionately as we might; we must impose gratuitous suffering on the terminally ill.

A third argument often comes from patients severely deprived and dependent or persons dreading the prospect of such a condition: they do not want "to be a burden to others." This argument appeals, once again, to the moral importance of liberty: one rejects dependence out of pride. It also reflects the power of compassion. But the roles of the players reverse as a work of compassion. In this case, the patient wants to die out of compassion for the caregivers — to relieve them of the terrible burdens of giving care and the daily limitations upon their liberty. Since, moreover, awareness that she is a burden compounds the patient's own suffering, active euthanasia or assisted suicide appeals twofold as an act of mercy: it mercifully relieves caregivers of their burdens and patients of being a burden.

The fourth and fifth arguments surface not in the terms themselves but in associated rhetoric and literature. The fourth rests on
the conviction that dying is a private, personal, intimate event, at
most a matter for the patient in relation to his or her family, friends,
or physician. The public and its political representatives have *no*
compelling interest that justifies regulating or interfering in this
private event.

The fifth argument overlaps the first, deriving from an insistence
upon the patient's autonomy, growing specifically out of the fear of
losing control — control that a "how to" book on killing oneself or
arranging assistance in suicide seems to reinstate. This last argument
reflects the very American (and perhaps broadly modern) compulsion
to control one's life from which the large number of "how to" books
lining the shelves of every drugstore, bookstore, and library in the
nation seek to profit. Americans prize their independence and abhor
dependency and loss of control. Hence the popularity of such a book
as Derek Humphry's *Final Exit,* which invites people to reassert total
control over their lives, even over the last gasp of suffering, by helping
them design their own death. Furthermore, opening up the option of
active euthanasia also helps to restore a sense of control to some
physicians who have seen their powers reach an intractable limit in
patients whom their remedies cannot heal.

Voters, Judges, and Jurors

These arguments for euthanasia failed to persuade citizens of two
states — Washington and California — to decriminalize the practice. In one of these states, it appeared that the initiative would pass
by approximately 56 to 44 percent of the vote. But then Dr. Jack
Kevorkian, the zealot for euthanasia, inconveniently killed two
patients requesting his help the weekend prior to the election. The
sobering specificity of these two deaths appears to have reversed the

expected vote on election day. Derek Humphry and other leaders in the euthanasia movement were not pleased with Kevorkian's timing. (In effect, strategists and adventurists in the euthanasia movement had a falling out, not the first time this sort of thing happened in the unfolding of a cause.)

However, in the election of 8 November 1994, a bare majority of citizens in the State of Oregon (51 to 49 percent) approved Measure 16, which allows terminally ill patients to obtain a prescription for lethal drugs to end their lives. The particulars of Measure 16 include the following: the patient initiating the request must be capable[2] and a resident of Oregon, and an attending and a consulting physician must have determined that the patient suffers from a terminal disease. The disease must be incurable and irreversible, and the patient must be expected to die within six months. Fully informed and uncoerced, the patient must make the request orally at least fifteen days before the attending physician writes out the lethal prescription and in writing at least forty-eight hours before. A consulting physician and at least one of two other witnesses not related by blood or interest to the patient must sign off on the procedure. If, in the opinion of the attending or the consulting physician, a patient suffers from a psychiatric or psychological disorder or from depression that impairs judgment, either physician must refer the patient for counseling. In such cases, no medication to end the patient's life may be prescribed until the person performing the counseling services determines that the patient does not suffer from any of these disorders.

2. The measure specifies that a patient is "capable" if, "in the opinion of a court or in the opinion of the patient's attending physician or consulting physician, [he or she has] the ability to make and communicate health care decisions to health care providers, including communication through persons familiar with the patient's manner of communicating if those persons are available." Both the particulars of Measure 16 and the quotations in the text come from the *Official 1994 General Elections Voters Pamphlet — Statewide Measures Oregon.*

The measure includes additional safeguards protecting informed consent. The attending physician must inform the patient of "(a) his or her medical diagnosis; (b) his or her prognosis; (c) the potential risks of taking the medication to be prescribed; (d) the probable result of using the medication to be prescribed; [and] (e) the feasible alternatives, including, but not limited to, comfort care, hospice care and pain control." The patient must reiterate his or her original oral request after a lapse of fifteen days, and he or she retains the right to rescind the request at any time without regard to his or her mental state. The law also requires documentation of the process in individual cases on at least seven points and provides for collection, reviews, and statistical reports on the information by the state's Health Division.

Measure 16 also answers some of the major objections the health care community raises to legislation controlling active euthanasia and assisted suicide. "No professional organization . . . or health care provider, may subject a person to censure, discipline, suspension, loss of license, loss of privileges, loss of membership or other penalty for participating or refusing to participate in good faith compliance with this Act." Thus, doctors cannot be coerced to prescribe drugs for ending the life of patients. Further, the measure restricts the doctor to prescribing, not administering, the drug to the patient. This limitation brings the doctor up to the edge but does not wholly medicalize the act. It allows the sponsors of the measure to deny that the physician engages directly in active euthanasia or assists suicide. "Nothing in this Act shall be construed to authorize a physician or any other person to end a patient's life by lethal injection, mercy killing or active euthanasia. Actions taken in accordance with this Act shall not, for any purpose, constitute suicide, assisted suicide, mercy killing or homicide, under the law."

Oregon doctors who supported the measure thereby broke with the national office of the American Medical Association, which opposed it. The Oregon Medical Association decided to remain neutral in the absence of consensus among its members. The Oregon measure, unlike its failed predecessors in Washington and California, shrewdly restricted doctors to prescribing, not administering, the lethal drugs. However, the Catholic Church saw the prescription of lethal doses as "a half step from euthanasia."[3]

In reaction to the passage of Measure 16, a group of physicians, terminally ill patients, and residential care facilities sued the State of Oregon.[4] Plaintiffs argued that Measure 16 violates the Equal Protection and Due Process clauses of the Fourteenth Amendment because it does not sufficiently guarantee that the choice to end life will be both informed and voluntary. They also argued that the Measure infringes upon health care providers' freedom of association and freedom to exercise their religious beliefs. They sought an injunction against implementing and enforcing the Measure on the grounds that the "public interest in protecting vulnerable citizens from irreparable harm was greater than hardship to terminally ill patients who want the option of physician assisted suicide to be immediately available."[5]

Judge J. Hogan of the United States District Court, D. Oregon, granted a preliminary injunction on December 27, 1994. The injunction was upheld on appeal, and Measure 16 was ruled unconstitutional 3 August 1995, on the grounds that the measure unfairly discriminates against the dying. The appellate court agreed with the plaintiffs that the law violates the equal protection clause of the Constitution's Fourteenth Amendment. Michael Vernon, an AIDS patient, promptly announced that he planned to appeal the ruling. The Associated Press reported him as saying, "What about my Constitutional rights? I'm not asking anybody to do anything to anybody else. . . . I'm simply asking for the right of self-determination, and I thought our Constitution granted those things."[6]

3. As reported by Timothy Egans, *New York Times*, 25 November 1994, pp. A1, B4.
4. *Lee v. State* 869 F.Supp. 1491 (D.Or. 1994).
5. *Lee v. State*, 1492.
6. Vernon, as quoted by William McCall, *Boston Globe*, 4 August 1995.

Judge Stephen Reinhardt of the Ninth Circuit Court of Appeals (sitting in California) indirectly answered Michael Vernon's question about his constitutional rights on Wednesday, March 6, 1996, by striking down a Washington State law that had made physician-assisted suicide a felony. The Court said that the law violated the Fourteenth Amendment's implicit guarantee of personal liberty to terminal patients. A month later, on April 2, 1996, the Second U.S. Circuit of Appeals struck down parts of a long-standing (1828) New York State ban on assisted suicide, by appeal once again to the Fourteenth Amendment. In this case, however, the judges grounded their decision not on the personal liberty of terminal patients but on their right to equal protection under the law, also guaranteed by the Amendment. They reasoned that some terminally ill patients already had the right to hasten their death legally by withdrawing treatments, but other terminal patients were deprived of that right by New York's legislative ban on assisted suicide, and in this way they were denied equal protection under the law. Specifically, the Second Circuit Court ruling states that New York "does not treat similarly circumstanced persons alike: those in the final stages of terminal illness who are on life-support systems are allowed to hasten their deaths by directing the removal of such systems, but those who are similarly situated, except for the previous attachment of life-sustaining equipment, are not allowed to hasten death by self-administering prescribed drugs."[7] In effect, this judgment, if sustained, would collapse the distinction between allowing to die and assisted suicide. The Court would see no difference between withdrawing treatments deemed pointless and supplying patients with the means to kill themselves.

The Supreme Court, as of this writing, has not yet ruled on the

7. *Timothy E. Quill v. Dennis C. Vacco,* heard before the U.S. Court of Appeals for the Second Circuit, No. 60 — August Term, 1995, Decided: April 2, 1996, Docket No. 95-7028.

decisions of the two Circuit Courts of Appeals. But these decisions could well supply the blueprint for subsequent rulings by other federal appeals courts and perhaps by the Supreme Court itself. Were the Supreme Court to side with Judge Reinhardt, it would create, according to Prof. Kathleen M. Sullivan of Stanford University Law School, "a sweeping new liberty interest . . . the first extension of a right to privacy since Roe v. Wade."[8] Alternatively, of course, the Court might declare the Constitution silent on the issues of active euthanasia and assisted suicide, in which case the Court would, in effect, leave these matters to state-by-state decisions.

Measure 16 did not entirely escape criticism from the quality-of-life camp. Dr. Kevorkian has criticized the Oregon law because it restricts dying by doctor's prescription to the last six months of life. He argues that this restriction fails to provide adequately for assisted suicide. The patient's quality of life, not the imminence of death, should determine the appropriateness of the decision, and the decision should be solely in the hands of the patient and doctor. Moreover, Kevorkian believes that physicians should be free to administer, rather than merely prescribe, the fatal drugs. Doctor-assisted suicide is a purely medical procedure, says Dr. Kevorkian, who calls it "medicide."

Kevorkian's language is intemperate. When his twenty-first patient since June 1990 (Margaret Garrish, seventy-two) appealed on television for either pain relief or "a way out," two doctors responded with offers to treat her pain. Dr. Kevorkian dismissed them as publicity seekers. He has also referred to those who have sought to enforce a Michigan law banning assisted suicide as "immoral idiots" and "Nazis masquerading as law enforcement types."[9] Still, despite his actions and his outbursts, no fewer than three juries have now acquitted Dr. Kevorkian of criminal acts either under

8. Sullivan, quoted in the *Washington Post,* 9 March 1996, pp. A1, A13.
9. Kevorkian, quoted by McCall, *Boston Globe,* 29 November 1994.

explicit Michigan legislation prohibiting assisted suicide or under the common law tradition of the state.

Thus, voters, judges, and jurors have now added their more temperate voices to those of Humphry and Kevorkian, calling for a huge change in our practice toward the dying.

The Arguments Against

Opponents of policies that would regularize the option of active euthanasia or assisted suicide have grounds for skepticism about each of the five arguments in their favor. As proposals like Oregon's Measure 16 appear across the nation and citizens divide almost evenly over instituting these policies, it behooves us to consider the arguments to the contrary.

1. Respect for the Autonomy of the Dying

Behind the emphasis on the voluntariness of the act of dying lies what Richard McCormick, S.J., has called the "absolutization of autonomy."[10] Libertarians insist on the unconditional right of self-determination (except for those actions that would either limit the freedom of others or harm them without their consent). They believe that an action is validated solely by the fact that someone has chosen it. Imposing is the chief sin. The power of the state should be minimal. Following this commitment to its logical limit in the political order, "absolutist" libertarians would urge repealing laws against all consensual acts of killing — not only voluntary euthanasia and assisted suicide but also dueling. Given their assump-

---

10. McCormick, "Physician-Assisted Suicide: Flight from Compassion," *Christian Century*, 4 December 1991, p. 1132.

tions, they could not even offer any reasonable grounds for prohibiting slavery should an enslaved person consent to his or her own degradation.

Not all libertarians seek to embody their theories in such extreme laws, but they do tend to honor men and women simply as individuals and neglect the doubleness of human existence. We *are* individuals, to be sure, but we are also parts of a whole. The society has an interest in us not simply when we harm others but also when we harm ourselves — an interest that grows in proportion to the magnitude of the harm. As Daniel Callahan wryly observed, "Consenting adult killing, like consenting adult slavery or degradation, is a strange route to human dignity."[11] We should not confuse respect for a person and his dignity with a readiness to permit or assist him to do whatever he chooses. Readiness to accede to the wishes of another does not always reflect respect, and a refusal to respond favorably to such requests does not always betray disrespect.

Further, the practice of voluntary euthanasia — viewed as an expansion of the patient's right to determine his or her own destiny — may reflect an extremely naive view of the uncoerced nature of the decision. The decision and plea to be killed is hardly an unforced decision if the terms and conditions under which we deliver care for the dying is already woefully mistargeted, inadequate, or downright neglectful. When elderly patients have stumbled around in apartments alone and frightened for decades, when they have spent years warehoused in geriatrics barracks, when they have not been visited by relatives for months, or when relatives dump them in emergency rooms to be rid of them for a holiday and they then ask to be killed for mercy, this can hardly be characterized as uncoerced. Their alternative may be so wretched, repellent, and distasteful as to push some patients toward this death to resolve their plight.

11. Callahan, *Hastings Center Report,* March-April 1992, p. 52.

Patients may feel pressure to kill themselves or to let themselves be killed for reasons other than an inadequate health care system. Herbert Hendin, M.D., has carefully reviewed both a Dutch film, *Death on Request,* about a patient suffering from amyotrophic lateral sclerosis, and a lengthy *New York Times* article about a Seattle woman suffering from an unnamed degenerative neurological disease whose death was arranged by her doctor and the head of Compassion in Dying, a group that presses for legalizing assisted suicide.[12] Hendin notes that even these hand-picked cases, designed to showcase assisted suicide as an expansion of patient autonomy, provide evidence of the sort of coercion that health caregivers, family members, and intimates can impose on a patient. Once assisted suicide is on the table and a patient makes a preliminary decision, a momentum takes over: preparations begin, the expectations of intimates build up, and a spouse may subtly withdraw from contact with the patient. Physicians, to be sure, may pose the question of assisted suicide a second time with a patient, to confirm the patient's consent, but they may fail to do so in a private meeting with the patient, under circumstances that would give the patient more freedom to reverse himself. Thus, the deadline acquires an unwanted definiteness, and the role of caregivers shifts from simple solidarity with the patient to that of managers of an event that the patient has not fully owned. The lifting of a prohibition does not automatically expand liberty.

Dr. Hendin, who also serves as executive director of the American Suicide Foundation, notes, in a comment on the case of Myrna Lebov, that "chronically ill and dependent people who say they want help in committing suicide are not always acting out of free choice."[13] Ms. Lebov, suffering from multiple sclerosis, secured her spouse's help in taking enough antidepressants to kill herself. On the surface, it looked like a case of purely voluntary assisted suicide,

12. Hendin, "Dying of Resentment," *New York Times,* 21 March 1996, p. A25.
13. Hendin, "Dying of Resentment," p. A25.

until a passage from her husband's diary was disclosed: "You are sucking the life out of me like a vampire and nobody cares."[14] Citing a 1983 study, Dr. Hendin observes that in the Netherlands, "more requests for euthanasia came from families than from patients." Even more worrisome, notes Dr. Hendin, is the fact that the acceptance of euthanasia as a practice in the Netherlands has reduced the interest there in relieving pain and suffering — a result that surely increases, in turn, the pressure to seek one's "out" through euthanasia and assistance in suicide.

2. Compassion toward the Dying

It is a huge irony and, in some cases, hypocrisy to urge a compassionate killing when we have starved the aged and dying for compassion for many of their declining years. To put it bluntly, a country has not earned the moral option to kill for mercy in good conscience if it hasn't already sustained and supported life with compassion and mercy. Active euthanasia could become a final solution for handling the problem of the aged poor. (Over forty million citizens of the United States lack health care insurance. It is the only industrialized country other than South Africa that so denies a major portion of its citizens acute care. Active euthanasia might provide too many people an offer they might feel, given the alternative, that they could not refuse.)

Further, the test of compassion lies not in investing yet more money in acute-care facilities (the United States already spends too much on such facilities) but rather in shifting substantial amounts of resources to preventive medicine, rehabilitative medicine, long-term and terminal care, and strategic home services that would provide patients with a humane alternative to a quick death. Other-

14. Hendin, "Dying of Resentment," p. A25.

wise our society cumulatively kills not for compassion but for con-venience — and to reduce the demands on our compassion. By denying adequate provision for chronic care and home assistance, our society nudges not only the solitary, neglected patient toward the exit but also the patient who watches his old, tired, and over-burdened mate painfully attempt to give him care without any humane respite. In saying this, I am not questioning the motives or the compassion of doctors or family members in specific cases; I am suggesting that the test of compassion is not simply the individual case but the cumulative impact of a social policy.

Admittedly, this argument is partly culture-specific. Other socie-ties provide for the stricken and the elderly more adequately than the U.S.A. does; and one such country, the Netherlands, also pro-vides legal accommodation for active euthanasia in those instances when persons may opt out of that care. But we should hesitate to make legal provision for a form of care that simply provides a convenient final solution for a society's general carelessness.

While this argument is culture-specific at the level of policy, how-ever, it is not relativist at the level of moral principle. It argues that our social covenant obligates us to provide care always. Most of the time, this care will take the form of treatment, though at some point treatment may no longer serve the patient's well-being. But in such cases, even when we cease to treat, our social covenant requires that we continue to care. Unceasing care is the moral principle behind passive euthanasia (i.e., allowing to die). Admittedly, we can abuse passive euthanasia, as I conceded at the outset. No line-drawing solves all problems. The proper use, as distinct from the abuse, of passive euthanasia depends upon the degree to which the act of letting die reflects the covenantal principle of care.

A mirror-image cruelty, however, would occur if one refused to perform a merciful procedure, clearly in the interest of a patient, merely in order to pressure the society to provide adequate alternative care for the aged, the comatose, and the terminally ill. Thus, laws prohibiting active euthanasia should be accompanied by laws permitting a full and proper use of passive euthanasia. Patients' welfare and their rights to refuse treatment should govern not only starting the machines but also stopping them, not only withholding treatment but also withdrawing it, not only using extraordinary means but also using ordinary means. Otherwise an acceptance of passive euthanasia could lead to inappropriate treatment and patient abuse.

Before the 1980s, both doctors and hospitals tended to define allowing to die too restrictively. Doctors exercised discretion in starting machines, but, once the machines began to whir, they could not stop them. They could refrain from taking heroic measures, but they were obliged to use all "ordinary measures" (such as dosing the about-to-die patient with penicillin that "cured" his pneumonia and dragged out his dying). Further, hospitals recognized no obligation either to establish policies governing the care of the dying or to inform patients and their families about them. In the absence of such policies, custom ruled physicians and hospitals, placing them under unspoken contract to fight unconditionally against death.

The first institutional breach in this very restrictive understanding of allowing to die came in 1976, when the Clinical Care Committee of the Massachusetts General Hospital (MGH) published an article in the *New England Journal of Medicine* entitled "Optimum Care for Hopelessly Ill Patients."[15] The Ethics Committee distinguished between maximal treatment and optimal care and emphasized that maximal treatment did not always constitute optimal care for the dying patient. The standard of optimal care should govern decisions not only in starting machines and taking heroic measures but also in stopping machines and resorting to such ordinary treatments as penicillin. In the same issue of the *New England Journal*, staff members of Beth Israel Hospital, Boston, published an article agree-

15. "Optimum Care for Hopelessly Ill Patients," *New England Journal of Medicine* 295 (1976): 362-64.

ing substantively but disagreeing procedurally with the MGH policy statement. In an article entitled "Orders Not to Resuscitate," the authors from Beth Israel Hospital complained that the MGH statement served as a guide to professionals only and failed to provide for the participation of patients and their families in these weighty decisions. Beth Israel established procedures for patient and family consent to treatment.

Later, in the early eighties, the President's Commission for the Study of Ethical Problems in Medicine and Biomedical and Behavioral Research published a report entitled *Deciding to Forego Life-Sustaining Treatment*[16] that answered the question of whether anything good can ever come out of Washington. The report provided the intellectual basis for later federal regulations requiring all hospitals that receive federal funding to develop policies on the care of the dying, to make them known to patients and their families, and to provide for their participation in basic decisions governing care. For the most part, institutions have responded to the regulations by preparing advance-directive documents that patients can use to specify what sorts of treatment they would like to receive in a variety of medical contexts. Such devices as living wills and durable powers of attorney have also been used to dictate the intentions of patients and their families. Yet these expressed wishes are not always fully acted on. In an article in the *Journal of the American Medical Association* in 1995, Dr. R. Sean Morrison reported that a large teaching hospital in New York failed to recognize, for various reasons, the documented instructions of advanced geriatric patients in 133 out of 180 reviewed cases.[17] Of 53 patients who lost the capacity

16. President's Commission for the Study of Ethical Problems in Medicine and Biomedical and Behavioral Research, *Deciding to Forego Life-Sustaining Treatment: A Report on the Ethical, Medical, and Legal Issues in Treatment Decisions* (Washington: U.S. Government Printing Office, March 1983).

17. Morrison, *Journal of the American Medical Association* 274 (9 August 1995): 478-82.

to make decisions while hospitalized, the hospital failed to recognize and/or honor 39. Too often patients treat the advance directive as a pro forma document, discussing it only with the doctor or a spouse but not with their whole family. And some doctors are reluctant to act on orders — even signed orders — if they sense disagreement within the family.

The combined reluctance of the medical profession and specific institutions and/or the inertia and confusion of families often delay decisions to stop treatment. Until the last few days of life, the manic standard of maximal treatment tends to determine decisions about all except extremely old patients. Leaders in the Hospice movement complain that doctors either fail altogether to refer patients to the local hospice or refer them when it is too late for the hospice to help them and their families through the ordeal of dying. Our system seems to condemn the terminal patient to helplessness or to maximal treatment, while the merry-go-round of maximal medicine whirls on.

Expanding the doctor's discretionary power to allow the patient to die does not of itself address the pain and suffering of the dying patient. Thus prohibitions against active euthanasia and assisted suicide impose an even more intense responsibility on the doctor to make sure that no patients, especially those who are being allowed to die, are abandoned to pain. As efforts to treat are relinquished, efforts to care for, make comfortable, and console must intensify. In a fine appendix to the Commission's volume, Dr. Joanne Lynn, a distinguished hospice physician, specified some of the details of humane care that our obsession with spectacular TV medicine has tempted us to neglect: using drugs effectively to control pain; adroitly managing various gastrointestinal, respiratory, and agonal symptoms; treating skin problems, fever, and weakness; and encouraging mental alertness.[18] These prosaic tasks, which high-tech

18. Lynn, "Appendix B: Supportive Care for Dying Patients," in *Deciding to Forego Life-Sustaining Treatment,* pp. 275-97.

medicine has tended to dismiss as hand-holding, are essential parts of the modest covenantal efficaciousness of care.

Some people fear using drugs such as morphine to control pain on the grounds that they are addictive and eventually hasten death (inasmuch as they tend over time to shut down the organ systems of the terminally ill). But many theologians and health care practitioners have accepted their use and distinguish that use both from the slavery of addiction and from active euthanasia. Why worry about addiction in the terminally ill if it relieves pain? Their addiction to a pain-relieving drug exacts a price without a consequence. Further, the hastening of death is a morally acceptable "double effect" of the drug's use so long as one administers the drug solely to relieve pain and not to hasten death. Hastening death, in such cases, is an anticipated but unintended result. The administration of a drug in doses sufficient only to relieve pain, even if those lower doses have the secondary effect of shortening the life of the terminally ill patient, differs morally from the delivery of an overdose deliberately to kill. (Dr. Kevorkian has seized upon this traditional doctrine of double effect to evade conviction for violating a Michigan law against assisted suicide. He has insisted that when he helps patients breathe carbon monoxide, he intends only to relieve their suffering [which the law permits] and not to cause their death. Of course, he has glossed over the fact that carbon monoxide categorically differs from a drug like morphine in that it offers no relief from suffering except by killing!)

Medical research and education have not yet focused sufficiently on the pressing needs of the dying. As Dr. Lynn elsewhere complained, "Often 'it is easier to get a heart transplant or cataract surgery than supper or a back rub,' let alone effective pain relief."[19] Dr. Kevorkian can engage in overtreating his patients with assisted

19. Lynn, quoted by Peter Steinfels in the *New York Times*, 14 February 1993, sect. 4, pp. 1, 6.

suicide because he attracts those who have been undertreated for depression. Apparently the zealous missionary never bothered to have the first nine of his patients psychiatrically evaluated before he helped them die. A 1991 *New England Journal of Medicine* editorial noted that 90 percent of the 30,000 people who committed suicide during the previous year in the U.S.A. suffered from depression. "One study of 45 terminally ill patients showed that only three patients considered suicide, and when they were examined psychiatrically, it was discovered that they suffered from major clinical depression."[20] But the estimated rates of failure to diagnose both minor and major clinical depression by primary care physicians range from 45 to 90 percent.[21] We generally underevaluate, and thus mistreat, the dying. Some 81 percent of doctors conceded in a survey reported in a *New York Times* editorial that "the most common form of narcotic abuse in the care of the dying is the undertreatment of pain."[22] Only one in ten physicians participating in a 1989 study conducted by Dr. Jamie H. Von Roenn of Northwestern University "said they received good training in managing pain."[23] Only one-fifth of 1 percent of the billion dollar budget of the National Cancer Institute goes to research on reducing pain. Instead of covenantally caring appropriately for the dying, the active euthanasia movement tempts us to swing smoothly from aggressive treatment aimed at keeping patients alive to equally aggressive treatment aimed at killing them.

20. Yeates Conwell, M.D. and Eric D. Caine, M.D., "Rational Suicide and the Right to Die," *New England Journal of Medicine* 325 (1991): 1105.

21. Leon Eisenberg, "Treating Depression and Anxiety in Primary Care," *New England Journal of Medicine* 326 (1992): 1080-84.

22. *New York Times,* 25 January 1993.

23. Cited by Richard A. McCormick, S.J., in "Physician Assisted Suicide: Flight from Compassion," *Christian Century,* 4 December 1991, p. 1133.

3. Compassion for Caregivers

Some patients (many of them aging patients) argue for active euthanasia because they do not want to end up a burden others. At first glance, this argument seems far removed from the underlying individualism of those who argue for active euthanasia on the basis of the patient's autonomy. It reflects the moral sense that we are not merely individuals but parts of a larger whole. We do not want to trouble *others*. Far from making an imperial claim to autonomy, the person so disposed insists only on her freedom to make a decision that benefits others.

While not denying the self-sacrificial character of such a patient's sentiment or action, I question whether the total moral setting that gives rise to it actually reflects the sense that we are parts of a whole. I am truly and fully a part of a community not only when I am willing to make sacrifices for others but also when I am willing to accept their sacrifices for me. Community is a two-way street of giving and receiving, not giving alone. In some circumstances and stages of life, we are primarily givers; at other times we should not be too proud to be receivers. At its healthiest, community depends upon interdependence, upon a reciprocity of giving and receiving.

The very fact that a chronically dependent patient would consider attempting to relieve her overburdened caregivers through her own death suggests that her society is insufficiently supporting its caregivers or failing to provide them with adequate respite from their labors. The lack of social supports for home and long-term care reflects a society harshly atomistic in its thinking. It demands from the unlucky a level of sacrifice that only the most saintly could sustain. While we may admire the sacrificial responses of the disabled or the dying who would save members of their immediate circle from making heroic sacrifices, it is difficult to admire the moral commitments of a nation that would push individuals and families to such desperation.

4. The Privacy of Dying

The fourth argument defines dying as an intimate, private, at most familial act that ought not to be subject to public regulation and scrutiny. This argument overlooks the public element in human life from birth to death. Birth is our first caterwauling public appearance, and the funeral is our final ceremonial exit from the public scene.

A society cannot plausibly wash its hands of the practice of active euthanasia and say that the doctor's cooperation in killing is a purely private matter. A huge public investment supports training doctors and places medical resources at their disposal. Further, the very nature of the decision to euthanize perforce implicates the society in the deed. Daniel Callahan has analyzed the public dimension of the decision as follows: "If doctors, once sanctioned to carry out euthanasia, are to be themselves responsible moral agents — not simply hired hands with lethal injections at the ready — then they must have their own *independent* moral grounds to kill those who request such services."[24] A simple appeal to the patient's declaration that he or she suffers unbearably does not constitute independent grounds. Doctors experienced with the complexities of active euthanasia in Holland concede that "there is no objective way of measuring or judging the claims of patients that their suffering is unbearable."[25] The patient's declaration reflects not only the medical condition but the values of the patient as well. In effect, then, the doctor must treat the values of the patient in addition to the disease and the request to die. A doctor cannot responsibly accede to the request unless the doctor and patient share values. Inevitably, this transaction pushes the decision out into the public arena. "Euthanasia is not a private matter of self-determination. It is an

24. Callahan, *Hastings Center Report*, March-April 1992, p. 52.
25. Callahan, *Hastings Center Report*, March-April 1992, p. 53.

act that requires two people to make it possible, and a complicit society to make it permissible and acceptable."[26]

A number of lawsuits before various state and federal courts (in California, Michigan, and New York) are currently contesting laws prohibiting active euthanasia and assisted suicide on the grounds that they violate the constitutional right to privacy proclaimed in *Roe v. Wade*. Robert A. Burt of the Yale Law School worries about the effect of linking the issue of active euthanasia and assisted suicide to the Supreme Court's abortion decision. Prior to *Roe v. Wade*, abortion was widely recognized as a legitimate medical procedure, whereas physician-assisted suicide has not been legislatively endorsed anywhere in the United States except Oregon. For this reason, a Supreme Court decision that swept away legislative prohibitions against active euthanasia and assisted suicide would more drastically change the legal role of the doctor than *Roe v. Wade*. Moreover, an appeal to the privacy principle of *Roe v. Wade* would be particularly hard to limit. "The logical reach of the privacy principle does not stop with people suffering from imminently terminal illnesses. It would encompass any suffering whatsoever — physical or emotional in origins; intrinsically life-threatening in the short term, long term or never," says Burt. He goes on to note sardonically that "the poor, the elderly, unassertive, clinically depressed, members of disfavored minorities or some combination of all these" would most likely be abandoned to this constitutional right of privacy and "control" over their bodies.[27] While Burt expresses no enthusiasm for the Oregon law, he grants that at least the legislative route allows one to proceed by incremental steps rather than by the sweeping abstraction of a court decision.

But the appeal to the constitutional right of privacy figures in legislative arguments as well as judicial decisions and eventually makes

26. Callahan, *Hastings Center Report*, March-April 1992, p. 53.
27. Burt, "Death Made Too Easy," *New York Times*, 16 November 1994, p. A15.

it difficult to enforce constraints. Denying the public significance of dying intensifies the problem of the slippery slope (the thin edge of the wedge or the camel's nose under the tent — pick your own cliché). Advocates of active euthanasia, it should be acknowledged, argue that they have spread sand on the slippery slope. In the Netherlands, for example, the law requires that the patient's condition must be terminal and irreversible, with death imminent. The patient must also explicitly consent to his or her being killed. Only physicians can kill, and the killing requires the authorizing signature of at least two doctors. These various regulations serve to protect against the bizarre whims, the malice, or the neglect of third parties as well as against the sort of vicious, involuntary euthanasia practiced by the Nazis in the thirties and forties. Advocates have written similar protections for the procedure into the Humane and Dignified Death Acts proposed in the United States and Oregon's Measure 16.

It is difficult to imagine that a country as flat as Holland could produce a slippery slope. However, despite the country's many regulations governing active euthanasia, slippage has occurred.[28] Of the 130,000 deaths recorded in the Netherlands in 1990, some 6,000, or 4.6 percent of all deaths, were cases of involuntary active euthanasia — despite the fact that Dutch law prohibits it. (This figure includes not only the 1,000 explicitly identified cases of active involuntary euthanasia but also the 4,941 cases in which doctors report that they gave morphine not simply to relieve pain but for the express purpose of terminating life.) Further, "in 45% of the cases in which the lives of hospital patients were actively terminated without their consent, this was done without the knowledge of the families."[29] Of the 4,941 cases of morphine overdoses given with

28. For the following discussion, I have drawn on "The Report of the Dutch Governmental Committee on Euthanasia," 10 September 1991, as reported by Richard Fenigson in *Issues in Law and Medicine* 7 (Winter 1991): 339ff.

29. "The Report of the Dutch Governmental Committee on Euthanasia," p. 343.

the express intent to kill, 27 percent were done without a fully competent patient's knowledge; 60 percent of practitioners failed to consult another physician before killing without patient consent; and doctors, "with a single exception, never stated the truth in the death certificates." Physicians also flouted the rules governing voluntary euthanasia: 19 percent of physicians did not consult another physician; 54 percent failed to record the proceedings in writing; and 72 percent concealed the fact that patients died by voluntary euthanasia.[30] In reaction to this slippage, the Royal Dutch Medical Association has tightened the rules on the practice of active euthanasia. The new guidelines require doctors who take part in euthanasia to make an effort to have terminally ill patients administer the fatal drug to themselves whenever possible rather than having a doctor apply an injection or an intravenous drip. Further, the consulting doctor must not have a professional relationship with either patient or family. Finally, the new regulations state that no doctor is required to perform euthanasia — but those who are opposed on principle must make their position known to the patient promptly and help the patient get in touch with a doctor who has no moral objections.[31] These changes move Dutch regulations closer to guidelines found in Oregon's Measure 16, currently before the courts. In part, they reflect a need to make the rules more palatable to doctors.

The tendency of Dutch practice to slip from the moorings that the country's regulations originally supplied may have followed from appeals to the intimacy and privacy of the act of dying. The insistence that dying is a private act places it, in principle, beyond public regulation and control. In such a context, we have to wonder with Leon Kass

30. "The Report of the Dutch Governmental Committee on Euthanasia," p. 343.

31. Marlise Simons, *New York Times,* 11 September 1995, p. A3.

whether regulating euthanasia is even possible: for how can one insist that euthanasia is and ought to be a private choice, best handled privately between patient and doctor, and yet expect there to be appropriate oversight, public accountability, and control? Must we, can we, should we, rely solely on the virtue of . . . unregulated medical practitioners — to protect the exposed and vulnerable lives of the infirm, the elderly, and the powerless who, incapable of real autonomy, will be deemed by others to have lives no longer worth living or, more likely, no longer worth sustaining at great medical expense?[32]

Carlos Gomez observes that

to suggest that what transpires between a physician and a patient, even at the hour of the patient's death, is an entirely private matter is . . . to overlook the public institutional quality of the profession of medicine. . . . For all its necessarily private and intimate aspects, . . . [medicine is] necessarily a *public* enterprise. . . . The claim to a right to death at the hands of a physician is essentially a private claim to a public good.[33]

Please note: the slippery slope that concerns me here is not the one conventionally feared — the lethal slide from the early Nazi practice of active euthanasia to Hitler's later policies of genocide. The chief danger many nations face today is not a demonic, totalitarian, political ideology but marketplace seduction. We need fear less the dictator who makes us do what we do not want to do (as in George Orwell's *1984*) than the seducer who tempts us to do

---

32. Kass, in a foreword to Carlos Gomez, *Regulating Death: Euthanasia and the Case of the Netherlands* (New York: Free Press, 1991), p. x. This volume is the most extensive American study of the Netherlands practice available.

33. Gomez, *Regulating Death*, p. 134.

what we ought not to do (as in Aldous Huxley's *Brave New World*). We are probably less vulnerable to the bark of the dictator's command ("Kill them!") than to the sweet talk of money ("We've got better uses for that money than to make Grandpa's life bearable. Let him go and let's get on with it"). "If the Netherlands — with its generous coverage — has problems controlling euthanasia, it takes little effort to imagine what would happen in the United States"[34] with a population ravenously dedicated to its own quality of life.

Now just why is the slippery slope worth thinking about? One of the original justifications for voluntary euthanasia is control of one's own dying. But crossing the boundary from the voluntary to the involuntary means losing just that control. It means putting to death someone against his will or without his will. The rock pile at the bottom of the slope contradicts the justifying flowers at the top of the slope.

5. *The Control of Dying*

The fifth argument for active euthanasia reflects the American obsession with solving problems through technical and contractual control and a corresponding fear and resourcelessness in the face of the uncontrollable and unpredictable. We seek to overcome the loss of control during dying by controlling the exit.

This way of seeing the active euthanasia movement differs from the conventional perspective with which this chapter began. Conventionally, ethicists have discerned opposing moral drives behind modern aggressive medicine and the reactive movement of active euthanasia. The modern medical establishment sees the doctor as a fighter against death who mobilizes all the technological resources of the profession in a pitched battle against disease and death. In

34. Gomez, *Regulating Death*, p. 138.

effect, medicine seeks to remove the mark of mortality from our frame. In reaction, supporters of active euthanasia identify suffering, not death, as the supreme evil and are prepared to give up the battle against death — indeed, kill — in order to spare the patient who so chooses pain and suffering.

Alternatively interpreted, a single moral obsession drives both movements. Both seek compulsively to solve the problem of human existence through control. In their extreme forms, both the anti- and the pro-euthanasia movements are contractual. Both groups focus the professional's skills on one specified outcome, mobilizing resources in linear and technical fashion to secure a single end: control. Modern medicine springs from the larger attempt of modern science and technology to extend human control over nature — first, over the waywardness of the external environment and, more recently, over the contingencies of the human body itself. But the effort to control disease ultimately reaches a limit. It cannot eliminate the ineliminable, our mortality. Further, as medicine wages its unconditional fight against death, it hugely expands another human contingency, the pain and suffering of those whom medicine has kept alive. In response to this latter state of affairs, active euthanasianists seek to reassert human control by letting patients design their own death and therewith bring their pain and suffering to an end.

No response to this argument can dismiss the value of the modern attempt to control the natural world and human life. Few of us would voluntarily give up the amenities, the abundances, and the rescues from disease and untimely death that modern technology has given us. Few of us, moreover, would want to impose gratuitous suffering upon ourselves or others when we can, to some degree, reduce it.

But the ideal of absolute control — realized in either the controlling person or the society committed to unconditional control — is morally unattractive. In a confessional key, Daniel Callahan notes in his book *The Troubled Dream of Life* that "in most of my life, I want and demand a great deal of control. But I came to feel — though not at first clearly to think — that perhaps I ought not to want to be that kind of person. I came to notice that, in other parts of my life, my desire for maximum control has not always served me well. It did not create a person I could invariably admire."[35]

The impulse to control creates abundant ironies. Psychoanalysts have recognized that the person who insists on controlling everyone and everything is, in fact, out of control. The society that prides itself on dominating nature has succeeded in massively polluting its environment and poisoning its citizens' bodies. The society that urges total war against suffering and death often imposes worse suffering and more turbulent deaths upon its members. Yossarian remarks in *Catch 22*, "I'm going to live forever, or die trying." The medical establishment ought to aim at a good death, not at eliminating death.

As policy, Callahan recommends that the old question of when a patient is dying and thus a candidate for the abatement of lifesaving treatment should yield to the more appropriate question of the point at which lifesaving treatment should be abated to enhance the likelihood of a good death.[36] This latter approach would not eliminate absolutely all pain and suffering, but it would help avoid those evils that beset us when we claim the right to control our fate totally.

The subtitle of Callahan's book — *Living with Mortality* — nicely expresses the equilibrium we should seek. Manically aggressive medicine has sought control by seeking to eliminate *mortality,* but, in doing so, it has inflicted upon us longer lives and worse health, longer illnesses and slower deaths, longer aging and increased

35. Callahan, *The Troubled Dream of Life: Living with Mortality* (New York: Simon & Schuster, 1993), p. 117.

36. See Callahan, *The Troubled Dream of Life,* pp. 46, 200-202.

dementia. Meanwhile, enthusiasts for active euthanasia have sought control of suffering by opting out of *living*. We need to cultivate the virtues that allow us *to live with our mortality*.

As a first move in acquiring those virtues, we need to recognize that many of the problems that confront patients and their families do not admit of technical, pragmatic solutions. However, the lack of such solutions does not automatically condemn us to impotence before them. We sometimes assume, to our impoverishment, that events give us only two options: either controlling our lives or passively submitting to them.

Unfortunately, narrowing our options to control and passivity overlooks an important range of responses to defining issues and events in life — by which I mean the sorts of things that define or redefine who we are, such as the conflict between the generations, the intricacy of signals between the sexes, the birth of a child, and the ordeals of fading powers and death. At one level, such things pose for us problems of a technical, pragmatic sort. So far in this chapter I have emphasized the importance of such practical responses to imminent death as hospital (and home) policies that provide optimal care for the terminally ill, that have produced protocols for advance directives and durable powers of attorney, that bear on the withholding and withdrawing of treatments. But, at another level, the defining events in life ask us not simply "What are we going to do about them?" but the deeper question "How does one behave towards them?" How does one become and remain whole in the midst of them? This deeper question goes to the issue of one's core identity — both for the person suffering through such an event and those who help that person heal. It requires, as we shall note later, the vistas associated with covenantal perception — a prudence requiring both attentiveness and discernment. Such events do not yield altogether to our problem-solving maneuvers. No specific policy, strategy, contract, or behavior can dissolve them. As Simone Weil put it, "What could be more stupid than to tighten our muscles and set our jaws about the solution" of such problems? They must be *faced* rather than solved. They resemble a mystery more than a puzzle; they demand responses that resemble a ritual repeated more than a technique, as we learn how to rise to the occasion.

Such events are tinged with the sacred. Sacred occasions or holy days are set apart from other days. On such days, the ordinary canons of mastery and control do not work. "Take off your shoes: you are on holy ground." You are on turf where you are not in charge. Karl Barth once distinguished workdays from holidays by observing that on workdays we make things happen, whereas on holidays we let things happen. The letting-things-happen of the holiday is not a state of mere passivity, however. By "taking in" the sacred occasion — the puberty rite, the marriage, the public gathering, the day of atonement, the Good Friday service — we let the occasion, in a sense, do the work, as it defines us.

Serious illness and death (and other defining events in life) often resemble the holiday: they call for decorous response rather than control. And that response in turn calls for an important set of virtues, the first of which is patience.

The dying patient needs *patience,* but this virtue differs from the buffeted passivity of being a patient — triply passive to the ravages of the disease, the ministrations of the experts, and the regimen of the treatment. Patience calls for a purposeful willing and waiting in the course of letting be and letting go. As such, the virtue contrasts not only with the obvious passivity of the patient but also with the frantic busyness and the driven agendas of those who hover about the patients projecting the illusion of activity and control.

Such patience resembles the virtue of courage, but in the second of its two modes. We customarily associate courage with its more active mode of attack. Active courage takes on evils and confounds them. We look for that kind of courage in the soldier, in the physician, and in ourselves when dealing with problems that can be solved. But before the insoluble, we need the more "passive" variety of courage that Thomas Aquinas identified as endurance or perseverance. Such perseverance does not mean that the person will outlast the trouble. Sooner or later, she must die. But, armed with courage, she can die without being thrown into panic and scattered by her trouble. She can endure. That is courage, not in the battlefield, but in bed.

Such patience and courage rest on the virtue of discernment, which classical moralists called *prudence.* They defined prudence as the eye of the soul and sensed its priority among the virtues. In order to know what to do and how to behave, one has to sense what is going on. In the first turmoil of mortal illness, one may not yet have attained that attentiveness and discernment, especially at a technical level of diagnosis and prognosis. That is why, in a sense, the patient's first response will be patience, a purposeful and attentive willing and waiting. But at length the patient and others must sense and discriminate between what is needful and helpful and what is intrusive and irrelevant. Such discernment is crucial in decisions to refuse treatment and in that letting go which allows one to die. And, as patients move beyond the capacity for discernment, they will especially require that virtue in their caregivers, to be vicariously exercised on their behalf. Patients will depend on others to exercise discernment as they stop irrelevant treatments and purposefully wait and perdure as lovers, friends, children, or attendant strangers.

Close to death, the patient, in the jargon of the analysts, "decathects." She detaches from the earthly scene. Others about her will try to say their farewells, still wracked by their sins of omission and commission, but she has already withdrawn. From one view, this passage out of the world seems to annihilate all love, shatter all ties. From another view, it creates a huge crater, an open space for love, the benevolence of being itself, a virtue beyond the virtues, their source and root.

This terrible opening of love allows one to catch a glimpse of hope. We ordinarily diminish hope to its snake oil version. We want to buy and clutch in our hands the miracle rescue that will work for one in a thousand patients. As patients or their immediate caregivers, we hope the miracle will let us continue our lives on the basis of what we hold in our hands — life, money, family, friends, position. Such hope fears being left empty-handed, denied all tricks and resources, bankrupt, friendless. The religious tradition recognizes that hope does not begin with clutching at nostrums and straws or vanish into the terrifying empty-handedness of death but rather unfolds in the openhandedness of love. Hope rests upon nothing in our own hands or in the doctor's hands but rather casts us, whether we live or die, in God's hands. Such hope rests in that final openhanded equanimity that would uphold all thousand of the living and the dying.

Not only as the about-to-be-bereaved and the bereaved but also as the mortally ill, we ourselves will need to learn how to rise to the occasion of our own dying. The community needs its aged and dependent, its ill and its dying, and the virtues they sometimes evince — the virtues of patience, courage, discernment, benevolence, and hope — just as much as it needs those virtues in the agents of its care.

We might plausibly view the movement on behalf of active euthanasia as a religious recoil against all the medical busyness and officiousness with which we have surrounded death — all the tests and protocols and contingency plans and codes and charts and tubes. While fretting in our busyness to save a life or delay the dying, we may sense that we have profaned the man or the woman doing the dying. We may have refused to open ourselves to what is happening by frantically working to make things happen. But, ironically, the movement of active euthanasia seeks to halt all these furious efforts at control by employing one more device of control. In the end, it is control that we demand, not a breakthrough to existence and meaning beyond the urgencies of control.

I do not see this final criticism of active euthanasia as justifying in itself a prohibition of the practice. But it may help open the door to some responses to death that would make the prohibition a little more tolerable.

Taking the arguments cumulatively and on the whole, I favor social policies that would permit allowing to die rather than killing for mercy, policies that would allow caregivers and patients to recognize the moment in illness when it is no longer meaningful to bend every effort to cure or to prolong life, when it is fitting to allow patients to do their own dying with technical assistance in managing pain. This policy seems most consonant with the covenantal obligations of the community to care and of those of us in need of care to rise to the occasion.

I can, to be sure, imagine rare circumstances in which I hope I would have the courage to kill for mercy — when the patient is irreversibly beyond human care, terminal, and in extreme and unabatable pain. A neurosurgeon once showed a seminar group the picture of a Vietnam casualty who had lost all four limbs in a land mine explosion. The catastrophe had reduced him to a trunk attached to a face transfixed in horror. Had I been on the battlefield, I hope I would have had the courage to cross the boundary and kill this sufferer with mercy. But hard cases do not always make good laws or wise social policies. Regularized mercy killings would too quickly and cheaply relieve the community of its obligation to provide good care. Who ever said the moral life is easy?

By admitting the possibility of an exception to a general prohibition against active euthanasia, I probably will please relativists and trouble absolutists. At first glance, relativists and absolutists seem radically opposed to one another. Relativists deny and absolutists uphold the validity of moral principles. But at a deeper level, they resemble one another. Both believe that the existence of an exception or a counterinstance undercuts the validity of a principle. Relativists seize upon the exception as reason for dissolving the principle.

Absolutists deny the exception or counterinstances in order to sustain the principle. Both fail to recognize the wisdom of Aristotle's observation that moral principles are true *for the most part.* They have general, not universal validity. The existence of some exceptions to a principle does not of itself destroy its validity or the laws based upon it. The recognition of some territorial limits to a principle, as it yields to a more urgent consideration in a particular case, should not of itself blot out the territory the principle covers. The rare exception to the general prohibition against active euthanasia should not of itself undercut the moral considerations that underlie the prohibition.

Further, we should not always expect the law to provide us with full protection and coverage for what, in rare circumstances, we may need morally to do. Sometimes the moral life calls us out into a no-man's-land where we cannot expect total security and protection under the law. Were I ever to find myself in a situation in which I felt that I must euthanize someone, I would think it best not to seek advance legal protection but to proceed as best I could and eventually throw myself on the mercy of the court. As a practical matter, that would tend to minimize the number of instances of active euthanasia. All things considered, it is best that the practice be rare.

A Covenantal View of Professional Character and Virtue

To ask whether a society should permit and regularize procedures for active euthanasia is to question the wisdom of a specific social policy. But the issue of active euthanasia cannot be entirely separated from the character and virtues that we expect or hope for in professional caregivers. If we reduce the professional to a mere tradesperson offering a technical skill for sale in the marketplace, then no strictly professional reason will compel the professional to question the practice of active euthanasia. The professional will merely contract to sell a skill that, at the beck and call of the consumer, can either prolong or end a life. Further, the professional who is reduced to a skilled entrepreneur will have little motive to bear with, support, or sustain dying or severely impaired patients through their ordeals unless they have specifically contracted for these less definable activities. This would effectively compound the suffering of those whom we allow to die. If we continue to prohibit the practice of active euthanasia and if we would morally strengthen the professional's case for allowing to die, we need an adequate understanding of what it means to be a professional and the virtues that this calling requires.

We also need to attend to the question of character and virtue before we can hope to succeed in reforming the health care system. Changes in a system do not always lead to improvements if the ethos of the players in the system remains the same. For example, the current health care system has seen a substantial shift from fee-for-service to an annual-fee system, in which doctors (and hospitals) profit from the difference between the annual fee and the cost of services actually delivered. As mentioned earlier, fee-for-service medicine has led to overtreatment; managed-care medicine, relying on the capitation system, has led to undertreatment. A physician currently engaged in the effort to make managed care work has wryly remarked that greed drove up costs in fee-for-service medicine, and now greed is driving down services in the managed-care system. This observation should not lead us to dismiss the effort to improve a system, but it should remind us that changes in the ethos must accompany systemic reform.

A credible view of professional character and virtue ought to consider the whole of professional practice and not simply fit the needs of an argument on the limited subject of active euthanasia or the systemic issue of health care reform. Still, the policy debate over active euthanasia, growing as it does out of the ordeals of the severely impaired and the dying, should help test our understanding of professional character and virtue. Thus this interpretation of professional character and virtue will reflect on their implications for the dying.

General Remarks on Covenants, Obligations, and Virtues

A covenantal ethic, above all else, defines the moral life responsively. Moral action (such as selling, refraining, respecting, giving, and professing) ultimately derives from and responds to a primordial receiving.

Covenantal obligation in its ancient and most influential form — the biblical covenant — arises from the exchange of goods between partners that leads to a fundamental promise, which, in turn, shapes the future of both parties to the agreement. The scriptures of ancient Israel are littered with such covenants between men and women and between nations, but they are controlled and judged throughout by that singular covenant which embraces all others: the covenant between God and Israel.

The great covenant includes four elements. The first is a gift — the deliverance of the people from Egypt. The second is an exchange of promises (at Mt. Sinai). The third element is the shaping of all subsequent life in response to the original gift and the promissory event. God "marks the forehead" of the Jews forever as they accept an inclusive set of moral commandments by which they will live. These commands are specific enough to make the duties of Israel concrete (e.g., laws governing the protection of the weak and provision for the stranger) yet summary enough to require a fidelity that exceeds contractual, legalistic specification (e.g., "Love the Lord thy God with all thy heart . . ."). Fourth and finally, the biblical narrative marks out those ritual means whereby Israel returns regularly to the foundational events that shape her life (the dietary laws, the Sabbath, and the holidays). These elements variously appear in the horizontal covenants between sovereigns and subjects, treaties between nations, and the important covenant of marriage. For Christians, God's covenant with Israel structurally prefigures the inclusive covenant that will spread across the whole of humankind in God's Son.[1]

(The subsequent meaning of *covenant* has not always carried forward the biblical sense of the term. The word, indeed, has often referred to a variety of unsavory practices — real estate covenants that keep blacks or Jews out of particular neighborhoods or loyalty

---

1. William F. May, *The Physician's Covenant* (Philadelphia: Westminster Press, 1983), chap. 4.

to a professional guild that sometimes takes precedence over professional duties to patients and clients. However, the biblical covenant offers resources for criticizing such narrowness and exclusivity. God, the creative, nurturant, and donative source of all beings, establishes the primary covenant that measures all others. Loyalty to God, whatever its particular implications, requires loyalty to all of God's creatures. Thus the covenant that distinguishes Jews and Christians from others requires them at the same time to deal openhandedly with others — not only with familiars but also with strangers and the needy.)

The four-part covenantal story can illuminate the medical covenant and practice in two ways: it can throw light on basic principles that should shape practice, and it can highlight the character and virtues required in the practitioner. Until recently, theologians have concentrated chiefly on teasing out abstract principles. They have examined the quandaries that professionals face in the course of their practice and looked to the biblical covenant for principles that will help to resolve these quandaries. The obligation theorist Paul Ramsey, for example, defined "covenant fidelity" as the ruling principle in medical practice and then applied it to an extraordinary range of issues, such as experimentation on human subjects, high-risk therapy, organ transplants, genetic engineering, abortion, in vitro fertilization, and care of the dying. Ramsey believed that faith in a faithful promise-keeping God readily converts into a general canon of loyalty and a derivative principle of the sacredness of life. His approach led him, in his justly influential book *The Patient as Person*, to adopt the general position on passive and active euthanasia taken in the first chapter of this book.[2]

However, Ramsey spent little time in that volume on the biblical covenant except for a few paragraphs in his preface. He seemed

2. See Ramsey, "On (Only) Caring for the Dying," in *The Patient as Person* (New Haven: Yale University Press, 1970), chap. 3.

convinced philosophically and theologically that the basic moral commands (the third element in the covenantal story line) are statable as moral principles, relatively detachable from the Commander. The principle of loyalty now occupies the foreground, and the promise-keeping God fades into the background.

This uncoupling of sacred narrative and moral principles serves the Christian ethicist who wants to throw light on vexing moral issues in biomedicine specifically within the general framework of secular philosophical discussion. It also lets the Christian ethicist address the society at large and the professions in particular without divisive appeals to a particular religious commitment. Appealing to mediating principles, Christian ethicists can throw light on vexing moral issues in medicine without losing a larger professional societal audience, only some members of which share Christian belief. Meanwhile, the huge institutions, such as hospitals and nursing homes that deliver services to large numbers of people (oftentimes strangers) need policies based on general moral principles that will help produce behavior upon which not only practitioners but patients can rely. One tends to expect these standards to be relatively acceptable and independent of the accidents of personal biography, philosophical conviction, and religious disposition.

For these various reasons, we cannot dismiss the agenda for medical ethics of obligation theorists such as Paul Ramsey and James F. Childress.[3] Their principle-oriented theories have value both philo-

---

3. See Tom L. Beauchamp and James F. Childress, *The Principles of Biomedical Ethics*, 4th ed. (New York: Oxford University Press, 1994). This vastly influential book organizes the discussion of biomedical ethics around four principles — respect for autonomy, nonmaleficence, beneficence, and justice — which the authors then apply to the full range of problems likely to surface for practitioners and policy makers. However, Beauchamp and Childress do not wish to deny the importance of the virtues for practitioners (see their last chapter, "Virtue and Ideals in Professional Life") any more than I wish, by focusing on the virtues in this chapter, to deny the moral importance of principles.

sophically and religiously, and they serve variously a religiously pluralist and secular society dominated by large organizations in need of generalized standards. But I believe that a covenantal ethic must also attend to the question of the moral agent and his or her virtues. Covenanted men and women do not simply accept a set of rules and principles guiding their actions; they also bind themselves over in the course of an event that alters and continuingly defines their identity. At Mt. Sinai, God marked the forehead of the Jews forever; through baptism, Christians acquire their very name and identity. As covenanted people take up the particulars of their several vocations, their identity will display itself in the character and virtues that properly typify their practice. No ethic that adequately explores the medical covenant can focus simply upon the quandaries that emerge in medical practice and the bearing of moral principles upon those quandaries; it must also explore the identity and nature of those agents who profess medicine. Virtue theory is the name we give to ethics as it focuses on such questions of identity (or character) and virtue.

Principle-oriented moralists concentrate on the question "What should we do?" Virtue theorists pose a second question that lies behind the first: "Whom shall we be?" Practitioners' answer to the latter question of identity may more fatefully affect, for good or for ill, their actual practice than the articulation of the principles that obligation theorists associate with applied ethics.

What does it mean to be a physician, a nurse, a chaplain, or a social worker? Is the professional identity simply a hybrid, an aggressive mix of technician and entrepreneur, or something more? If the practitioner is simply a careerist who puts his or her skills up for grabs to the highest bidder, then answers to the question of truth telling, plug pulling, price changing, guild policing, and resource allocating will at best simply reflect the driving force of self-interest. The payment system under which physicians and nurses operate will drive decisions affecting the care of the dying. Fee-for-service physicians will tend to order acute care services at full throttle. Others, operating under a capitation system, will be tempted to undertreat. In either case, physicians may not rightly serve the dying patient. They will simply sell time and services, throwing in an occasional act of charity to polish the image and salve the conscience. Only in acknowledging his or her identity as a professional does the practitioner assume the full burden of the moral principles that obligation theorists emphasize and that define the services the dying person needs.

Professional Character

"To profess" means "to testify on behalf of," "to stand for," or "to avow" something that defines one's fundamental commitment — a covenant, if you will, that shapes and constrains the professor. Without that commitment, the practitioner is merely a careerist; in the old religious language, he or she has no calling. A professional aspires toward an as-yet-unspecified good that defines the professor and her practice. In contrast, a careerist merely uses her identity as a lawyer, doctor, or nurse for some other purpose. The Hippocratic Oath acknowledged the importance of a fundamental commitment when it exacted from the young physician the vow "I swear by Apollo Physician and Asclepius and Hygieia and Panaceia and all the gods and goddesses, making them my witnesses, that I will fulfill according to my ability and judgment this oath and this covenant. . . ."[4]

Lacking something akin to this commitment, the professional, as professor, vanishes or rots. The philosopher Alasdair MacIntyre has distinguished between the goods internal to a practice — such as

4. Ludwig Edelstein, *Ancient Medicine,* ed. Owsei Temkin and C. Lilian Temkin (Baltimore: The Johns Hopkins University Press, 1967), p. 6.

the arts of lawyering, healing, and preaching — and the goods external to a practice — such as the fame, reputation, or fortune that a practice may generate.[5] The love of money, reputation, and fame distracts; it focuses attention elsewhere. And, as it distracts, it corrupts; it neglects and compromises the professional good. If the careerist practices medicine, dentistry, the law, or nursing only for the money, then she has lost that single-mindedness, that purity of heart, which allows all else to burn away as the good of the practice shines through.

In Kingsley Amis's *Lucky Jim,* a pompous college history professor answers his phone, "History here." He speaks more than he understands. His line is on the mark. Better than "Historian here" or "Dr. Toynbee here," "History here" points to the activity, pure and simple, rather than to the office or to the attainment of the person. Surely that is what a distressed patient wants when he calls the doctor about a baffling symptom: "Healing here"; and that is what the distressed client or parishioner needs when calling the lawyer or priest: "Sanctuary here."

While the virtues are plural, one virtue reflects that covenanted unity of character in evidence when the activity professed has so taken hold as to burn away all else and let the good of the practice itself have free play. Scripture calls it purity of heart, which, as Kierkegaard pointed out, is "to will one thing."[6] This professional chastity, if you will, is not a state of purity free of errant impulses and temptations; rather, the professional who has attained it *qua* professional does not let these externals divert or block the activity itself of healing, lawyering, or engineering.

The secular term for this professional purity of heart is *integrity.*

---

5. MacIntyre, *After Virtue: A Study in Moral Theory* (Notre Dame, Ind.: University of Notre Dame Press, 1981), p. 178.

6. See James 4:8: "Purify your hearts, ye double-minded," and, later, Søren Kierkegaard's classic *Purity of Heart Is to Will One Thing* (New York: Harper & Brothers, 1938).

The virtue of integrity shines out in images of uprightness and wholeness. Integrity gets tested in the forward scramble for admission to professional schools, the competition for grades, and the jostling for jobs and promotion. Integrity has to do with moral posture: the upright professional refuses to put his nose to the ground, sniffing out opportunities at the expense of patients and colleagues. She equally refuses to bow before the powerful client or patient, influential colleagues, or outside pressures or rewards. To temptation she replies, "That's not my style." Integrity also signifies a wholeness or completeness of character; it does not permit a split between the inner and the outer, between word and deed. As such, it makes possible the fiduciary bond between the professional and the patient.

The completeness or roundedness of integrity differs from mere self-sufficiency. While referring to the self in its wholeness, integrity also points beyond the self to what the self professes — that is, the transcendent good that shapes the self and its activity. Integrity refers to the inclusive self, to be sure, but the self turns out to be ecstatic, pitched out beyond itself toward that which it professes. Appropriately, we say that the professional has lost his integrity when his core identity with that defining activity breaks asunder. The man may be called a doctor, but he has lost his calling as a doctor when he exploits his expertise for ends other than healing.

Purity of heart is to will one thing; that singleness constitutes the distinguishing character or integrity of the professional. Still, we need to display analytically the several ingredients in such willing and practice. Abraham Flexner, the mother of all reformers in medical education, identified six marks that distinguish a professional.[7] Flexner's six marks boil down, in my judgment, to three: intellectual,

7. See Flexner, "Is Social Work a Profession?" *Proceedings of the National Council of Charities and Correction, 42nd Annual Meeting, Baltimore, MD, May 12-19, 1915* (Chicago: National Council of Charities and Correction, 1915).

moral, and organizational. Each of these characteristics, in turn, calls for a primary enabling virtue. The intellectual mark requires prudence; the moral mark, fidelity; and the organizational mark, public-spiritedness.

The Intellectual Mark and the Virtue of Prudence

The professional's covenant opens out in at least two directions: the professional professes *something* on behalf of *someone*. The "something" is a complex and esoteric body of knowledge not available to everyone but to which the professional has direct access. This direct access to first principles distinguishes professional education from mere training. Trained people can perform specific routines, but, according to Flexner, they don't know *why* they perform them. They quickly lapse into undeviating patterns; they don't adapt or grow. A knowledge of first principles, however, lays the foundation for the professional's future growth.

The need for direct acquaintance with basic principles led Flexner to insist that professional education be located in universities and that the so-called proprietary schools, which offered mere training, be closed. He further insisted that medical education take place in a university setting, on the ground that a profession must, in some range of its work, engage in scientific research that expands the profession's knowledge base and thus serves its advancement and progress. Not all professionals need be researchers, he argued, but some must. Somewhere within the profession — usually at the university — the profession must support the research enterprise.

If the professional's intellectual mark consisted of scientific knowledge and no more, then the student might need little more than the virtue of *perseverance* to acquire it. While a humble virtue, perseverance is indispensable to the acquisition of scientific knowledge and technical competence under the trying conditions of lengthy professional education today. A young physician once conceded to me that medical school requires more stamina than brains. I liked him for saying it. He instantly became my primary care physician, because I thought he would have the sense to turn over my case if any complications required a referral. Most holders of Ph.D.s would have to confess the same about their own graduate education — it took more stamina than brains — though it also takes the virtue of modesty to concede that fact.

But healing is an art, not simply a science, and thus it requires something more than the virtue of perseverance. Additionally, the physician needs the classical virtue of *prudence,* which we might appropriately characterize today as attentiveness and discernment.

Contemporary medical literature offers little help on the meaning of the phrase "the healer's art" and therefore does not leave much room for the discretion of the practitioner or the virtue that cultivates discretion. When general practitioners and internists appeal to medicine as an art, they sound rather apologetic, as though they hope to clear out a little space for themselves in a field already crowded with scientists and medical specialists who have divided up most of the turf. Scientists, meanwhile, accept healing as an art only in the provisional sense that gaps in our scientific knowledge have not yet closed, temporarily requiring the leap of the imagination, the inspired guess. They assume that as these gaps close, the need for the intuitive leap will disappear.

Advances in the scientific aspect of medicine have, in a sense, made possible the increasing institutional moves in the 1990s toward managed care. As science, medicine requires, and has advanced, specialized and abstract investigatory work. Each medical specialty rests on its peculiar knowledge base, which provides a series of indicators that signal the presence of diseases that its technical interventions can affect. This specialized knowledge and activity systematically abstracts from the patient as a whole by ignoring the technically irrelevant. But it also leads to the codification of the indicators of disease, the markers of its progress, and the parameters for therapy. It therefore allows for the micromanagement of disease from a distance, providing confirmations of diagnosis and prognosis and justifying approvals or disapprovals of therapy. So who needs the art of healing?

But healing purportedly includes a further element. The healer must attempt not only to cure the disease but to address the illness of which the disease forms a part. As Dr. Eric Cassell has put it, "Disease is something an organ has; illness is something a man has."[8] The host may be incidental to the disease (sometimes, not always), but the host is rarely incidental to the state of illness. The healer who would "make whole" stricken, even dying patients cannot rest content with a specialized and abstract knowledge, as much as that may contribute to the enterprise. The healer must look at the whole patient as a *gestalt*, the full range of somatic and psychic structures disrupted by disease. Such a knowledge must ultimately unite and specify, situating the disease in a particular person and in his or her idiosyncratic social history. The knowledge resembles more the coordinations of an experienced fisherman scanning the sea or a hunter wary in the woods or a cook fully experienced in the kitchen than it resembles the reductions of a particular case to a general law.

Finally, the reconstructive activity in which the healer engages includes more than curing disease. The fully rounded work of healing reconnects the patient with herself and her condition and helps her recover her self-confidence. The treatment plan at its best offers a coherent total program for as much recovery or relief as a particular patient can achieve under the circumstances. Preventive medicine and chronic and terminal care require such artistic intervention just as much as acute and rehabilitative medicine.

The fully developed physician needs the virtue of prudence, since the physician's act of knowing and doing is artful as well as scientific.

8. Cassell, *The Healer's Art* (New York: Penguin Books, 1979), p. 48.

Because healing is a making and keeping whole, it requires that the healer be attentive to the whole person and discern what will serve the patient to whom she is covenanted. Ethical theorists who orient to principles sometimes tend to downgrade the importance of prudence as they rely on general moral principles rather than the concrete insight and discretion of the moral agent. Some theorists trivialize prudence into a merely adroit selection of means in the pursuit of ends, into a crafty packaging of policies. The virtue of prudence, to be sure, deals with fitting means to ends. But, as a virtue, it consists of much more than the "tactical cunning" to which Machiavelli and many in the modern world diminish the virtue. Thomas Aquinas noted, "In order that a choice be good, two things are required. First, that the intention be directed to a due end. . . . Secondly, that man take rightly those things which have reference to the end: and this he cannot do unless his reason counsel, judge, and command aright, which is the function of prudence and the virtues annexed to it."[9]

The ancients gave a primary place to prudence as the "eye of the soul." The medievalists ranked prudence as the first of the cardinal virtues on the grounds that "Being precedes Truth and . . . Truth precedes Goodness."[10] Diagnosis and prognosis precede apt therapy. One must discern what is there in order to be there for it. A relaxed and alert openness to being underlies both being good and producing the good in and for others.

The art of prudent discerning includes three elements, especially if one hopes to discern fully a human being: (a) *memoria* — being truly open to the past (rather than retouching, coloring, or falsifying it); (b) *docilitas* — defined not as a bovine docility but as an openness to the present, the ability to be still, to be silent, to listen and

9. Aquinas, *Summa Theologica*, I-II, q.57, a.5.
10. Josef Pieper, *The Four Cardinal Virtues* (Notre Dame, Ind.: University of Notre Dame Press, 1966), p. 4.

take in what makes itself present; and (c) *solertia* — a readiness for the unexpected, the novel, an openness to the future, a disposition sometimes in short supply in those who only too quickly subsume the new case under old routines.[11] This disciplined openness to the past, present, and future fairly summarizes what the distressed patient needs from the healer. The moral tradition that argued for it long precedes Freudian wisdom on the subject of the therapeutic relationship.

Such prudence demands much more than a facile packaging of what one has to say or do. *Discretio* presupposes metaphysical perception, a sense for what the Stoics called "the fitting," a sensibility that goes deeper than tact, a feel for the other and one's own behavior that is congruent with reality. Without discernment, the professional does not deal with the whole truth in diagnosis and prognosis — that is, with the truths of illness as well as disease. And without discernment, the professional does not mobilize the full power of healing, which exceeds that of laser, knife, and drug.

The need for prudence intensifies in the treatment of the aged and the dying. Both practitioners and the health care system have been stubbornly obtuse or culpably slow in discerning and responding to the specific needs of the aged and dying. Doses of a medicine appropriate for a younger patient may constitute an overdose for the elderly, in effect poisoning the patient, disturbing family caregivers, and dislocating arrangements for the patient's care. For instance, a dosage of an antidepressant drug suitable for a young and otherwise healthy patient proved too large a dose for a seventy-year-old man with severe weight loss from cancer. The patient began to see Arabs in the trees outside his hospital window and restraints were required to keep him in bed. The honest doctor ruefully admitted to the patient's son, "I'm afraid I poisoned your father,"

11. For a general account of *memoria, docilitas,* and *solertia,* see Pieper, *The Four Cardinal Virtues,* pp. 14-17.

and proceeded to "dry out" the patient in order to remove the Arabs from the trees and clear the way for more targeted drugs.

Titrating drugs is more difficult for the elderly than for the young, since the margin of error is smaller, both by way of excess and defect. A ninety-two-year-old woman needs Haldol to suppress the symptoms of paranoia. However, too much of the drug immobilizes her and produces Parkinson's symptoms; too little leaves her with so-called sundowning symptoms — hallucinations of cobwebs and the like that appear at sunset and thereafter, terrorizing her and keeping her from sleeping. The line is narrow. The doctor must carefully take in what is there in the particular case in order to do her any good.

A doctor successfully treats an elderly woman for her swollen ankles with a diuretic. For reasons that are not clear, the patient objects to seeing the same doctor again. At length, the daughter discovers the reason: her aged mother associates the doctor with the trauma of incontinence, which the diuretic, of course, exacerbated. The medical profession has slowly responded to the special complications of treating the elderly by establishing gerontology as a specialization. But even the newly acquired generalizations of the speciality do not relieve the healer of responsibility for attentiveness and discernment in the particular case.

The medical profession and the health care system have imprudently bombarded the dying with curative services as though they were not dying. Over 30 percent of the American health care dollar now pays for services in the last six months of life, guaranteeing that the terminally ill will die in the comfortless vicinity of machines. Or, should they live, we have so lopsidedly invested in acute care treatments that neither they nor our society can afford to provide for the quotidian services that the enfeebled survivors require. The contract to fight against death almost exclusively controls the research imperative in the United States. We devote very little research money to assisting patients to a more peaceful death. And even though the hospice movement makes available more appropriate services for the terminally ill, oncologists and hematologists (and families) are loath to make (or accept) referrals to a hospice. Prudence or discernment is the eye of the soul, but we find it difficult to keep the eye open in the face of the ultimate adversity. In behaving as though patients are not dying, we impose upon them medically the ultimate inattentiveness.

The Moral Mark and the Virtue of Fidelity

Professionals who stand for or avow something do so on behalf of someone. They profess not simply any and all knowledge but a particular body of learning that applies beneficially to a specific range of human problems. Unlike earlier knowledge merchants, such as wizards and magicians, who contracted to produce one thing or who used their knowledge simply to display their virtuosity, professionals must serve human need — and not simply their own needs or those of their friends and relatives but those of the stranger. "Hanging out one's shingle" has symbolized from the seventeenth century forward the professional's readiness to direct knowledge to the needs of the stranger.

The symbol of the shingle is ambiguous. It invites the stranger, but it does so, at least partly, in the setting of the marketplace. The professional differs from the amateur in that the amateur does it for love and the professional for money. Only a species of angelism would argue otherwise. Professionals are not disembodied spirits. They earn their bread and pay their bills in the course of serving others. The professional exchange with patients and with the institutions for which they work partly conforms to a marketplace exchange of buying and selling. It therefore requires the traditional marketplace virtues of industry, honesty, and integrity.

But the professional exchange also transcends, or ought to transcend, the cash nexus. It requires the further virtue of fidelity. A sustained and sustaining commitment to the being and well-being of the patient distinguishes the professional exchange from a marketplace transaction. Buyers and sellers in the marketplace meet as two frankly self-interested and relatively knowledgeable parties. Both sides are justifiably wary. However, patients cannot obey the marketplace warning "Let the buyer beware." Their very limited medical knowledge and often confused perception of self-interest hardly protect them. An asymmetry exists between the professional's knowledge and therefore power and the patient's relative ignorance and powerlessness; further, the patient's urgent distress often does not leave time for comparative shopping. This imbalance requires that the professional exchange take place in a fiduciary setting of trust that transcends the marketplace assumptions about two wary bargainers. Only the physician's fidelity to the patient in the disposition of his or her knowledge and power justifies that trust.

Fidelity to the patient should constrain the physician's notion of what he or she has to sell. If I walk into a Volvo showroom, I do not expect the salesperson to question whether I actually need a Volvo. No one in a Volvo showroom has ever suggested to me that, as an academic, I ought to trot across the street and buy at half the price a Toyota Tercel. The salesperson takes it as a challenge to sell me a car and thereby meet his quota for the month. I am a pork chop for the eating. But if I visit a surgeon, I must be able to assume that he or she sells two items, not one. The surgeon is not simply in the business of contracting to sell hernia jobs but is also covenanted to sell the detached, disinterested, unclouded judgment that I need that wretched little procedure. Otherwise, the physician abuses disproportionate knowledge and power and poisons a fiduciary relationship with distrust. Instead of sheltering, the surgeon takes advantage of the distressed.

Herein lies the ground for professional strictures against conflicts of interest. The professional must be sufficiently distanced from his or her own interests to serve the patient's well-being. However, serving the patient's welfare faces subtler pitfalls than gross conflicts of financial interest. For example, physicians must take care that they do not eagerly recruit their patients into high-risk research protocols at the expense of the patients' welfare. Otherwise, they act as double agents, pretending concern for their patients while serving, in fact, the drug or appliance companies or the advancement of their own careers as researchers. Fidelity requires disinterested discernment, judgment, and action on behalf of the patient's best interest and well-being.

The temptation to depart from disinterested fidelity to the patient takes two forms: overtreatment and undertreatment. The fee-for-service system generally tempts the practitioner to overtreat the patient, especially with acute-care interventions. Fee for service (a contracted piecework payment system) says, in effect, the more discrete pieces of work, the more compensation. Hospitals and doctors alike tend to dice up work into distinct, identifiable procedures, each qualifying for compensation, the cumulative effect of which, in the case of dying patients, is to overtreat them with acute-care services — precisely those services that the system can identify as separate, objective procedures. At the same time, the fee-for-service system tempts the practitioner to undertreat by failing to compensate adequately for those sometimes more thoughtful, sometimes less dramatic modes of care that the dying need. Recent adjustments in the federal fee schedules, which now pay less to the doers and more to the thinkers in medicine (less to surgeons, radiologists, and anesthesiologists, more to internists and deliverers of primary care) increase the rewards for the reflective work that the dying need. The fee-for-service system also fails to compensate sufficiently those many unglamorous caregivers who provide services for patients back in their homes or in nursing homes, where dying might more humanely take place. Disinterested professional service should not mean undercompensated professional service.

The current trends in the third-party payment system have moved the United States increasingly in the direction of undertreatment. The burgeoning growth of for-profit health maintenance organizations (HMO's) and preferred provider organizations (PPO's), which often contract to compensate physicians with bonuses based on the difference between a standard payment per patient and the cost of health services delivered, tends to encourage timely preventive medicine. Early treatment generally tends to reduce the overall costs of care. But the profit incentives that some HMO's and PPO's tie to reduced costs can tempt practitioners, hospitals, and delivery organizations to undertreat patients and thus compromise fidelity to the patient. This temptation affects not only the delivery of acute care but also some of those services that might reduce the suffering of the elderly, the dying, and their families. For example, some HMO's and PPO's will deny payment for adequate mental health services. (This omission led the American Psychiatric Association to state at its 1994 annual meeting that the psychiatrist has an ethical obligation to tell the patient [or family, in the case of the marginally competent] that a treatment is indicated, whether or not the HMO or PPO will approve of the care. But the HMO or PPO can often drop without cause the psychiatrist who has presented the organization with this awkwardness! Systemic pressures of this sort can make it difficult to practice the virtue of disinterested fidelity to the patient: a system that makes martyrs of those who practice ordinary virtue is, to say the least, somewhat faulty.)

The covenantal professional exchange differs in a second way from a contractual, marketplace transaction. In addition to its disinterestedness, it is, for want of a better word, transformational, rather than merely transactional. The healer must respond not simply to the patient's self-perceived wants but to his or her deeper needs. The patient suffering from insomnia often wants simply the quick fix of a pill. But if the physician goes after the root of the problem, then she may have to help the patient transform the habits that led to the symptom of sleeplessness. The physician is slothful if she dutifully offers acute care but neglects to look for the beginning of an illness and offer preventive medicine.

Rehabilitative medicine, long-term care, and terminal care also engage the healer in the task of transforming her patients. The victim of a heart attack, cancer, or a stroke suffers major changes in body and circumstance that reflexively call for changes in habits and skills in the course of rehabilitative and long-term care. The term "transformation," however, awakens legitimate fears of parentalism. The prospect of the physician engaged in transforming habits evokes memories of overbearing authority figures from the past. Transformational leadership slips into parentalism unless it teaches as well as prescribes. Teaching lets one engage in transformation while respecting the patient's intelligence and power of self-determination. No one can engage properly in preventive, rehabilitative, chronic, and even terminal care without teaching his or her patients and their families.

Thus fidelity to the patient in addressing his or her deeper needs brings the discussion back to the virtue of prudence. Prudence is sensitive not only to ends but to fitting means to those ends. The end of medicine is healing, but the art of healing must be applied to rational, self-determining creatures. In securing patient compliance with a regimen of acute care and the partnership of patient and family in the tasks of preventive, rehabilitative, and chronic care, the physician must honor fully the person who suffers the disease. The physician does not succeed in these tasks unless she learns from the patient in the course of the interview and teaches the patient aright in turn. Teaching the patient poses the question of how one should teach the sick and the stricken. If teaching is the means, what are the means to the means? How does one teach? Pedantically? Naggingly? Vindictively? Scoldingly? Scripture answers that question concisely: speak the truth in love. Therewith the virtues of prudence and fidelity knit together.

The dying patient has usually passed beyond the point of acquiring new habits, but fatal disease and dying often hugely alter the patient's perception of herself and her world. Professionals may not be able to transform by staving off the lethal disease or by changing long-established habits, but they can still make an important difference in the patient's and family's perceived world and therefore in their capacity to rise to the occasion. Healing, in the sense of keeping the patient and the family whole in the midst of dying, can help them persist and endure in the midst of assault. This task usually falls more heavily on nurses, chaplains, clergy, and workers in the hospice movement than on doctors.

Whoever provides such efficacious care to the dying needs the covenantal virtue of *courage*. Aquinas defined courage as the habit of keeping one's aversions and fears under control. Courage isn't fearlessness, a life free of aversions; it is a matter of keeping one's dislikes and fears under bridle for the sake of the good. It is firmness of soul in the face of adversity. Without such courage, the practitioner fails to secure the sort of detachment that is indispensable to the delivery of effective service. Most discussions of detachment emphasize the need to control one's wants and one's monetary self-interest for the sake of the alert and steadfast delivery of services. We have dealt with that necessity in our discussion of the need to deliver disinterested service. But it just as important that the social worker, the minister, the nurse, and the physician learn to control their frustrations with patients and their circumstances.

Aquinas further distinguished between active and passive courage — the active courage of attack and the passive courage of endurance. On the whole, we tend to associate professionals — the doctor, the lawyer, the engineer — with the more active, military virtue of attack. We seek out professionals when we face problems that overwhelm us, hoping that they command powers to banish or diminish our troubles. We especially look for this courage in those who deliver acute care medical services, people who will wade into the fray, despite wounds, smells, nasty symptoms, and risks, and do battle on our behalf.

Care of the dying, however, also demands that the professional display the passive form of courage: endurance or perseverance. The messiness of dying produces aversions, including an aversion to admitting limits to one's own powers and facing the indisputable sign, in the travail of another, of one's own eventual death. All professionals in the helping professions need, in some measure, endurance or resilience in facing the ordeals of others. When either the health care practitioner or the health care system as a whole denies that persevering presence to another in need and abandons the patient, the desertion at the bedside matches that on the battlefield.

This persevering presence with the patient has its limits, however. The dying patient, after all, is making an exit that begins before the end. As the patient withdraws, even the most adept professional and former intimates cannot fully track after her. Elisabeth Kübler-Ross, in her work on dying patients, overlooked this element of distancing that occurs in all authentic human relationships. In *Death and Dying,* she correctly criticizes professional strategies of avoidance but wrongly urges a kind of intimacy between the healer and the dying, a mystical merging of the two, that does not fully honor the complicated transparency/opaqueness of all human encounters, from the most intimate to the most crisis-laden. The more insightful Martin Buber remarked on the element of "othering" in the I-Thou relationship. Neither person in the meeting fully merges or submerges into the other. An element of strangeness marks the relationship of husband and wife, parent and child, patient and healer. One overlooks the other, fails to attend to or honor her, when one reduces her to the familiar and takes her for granted. I am never so attentive to others as when I see their otherness, never so neglectful as when I think I see through them and can afford to ignore them or when I reduce them to objects on whom I can practice my bag of tricks or my bedside manner.

Thus fidelity calls for a persevering presence to the dying, but the healer who accompanies must respect a traveler farther down the road. An easy familiarity, an effusive cheerfulness, a hit-and-run visit, or a routine pat on the shoulder too often reveals that the caregiver has long since turned his back on the dying. The decorum of being present is not easily come by. For one thing, a sense of decorum with the dying often moves caregivers beyond the glib expertise of words. The dying patient passes beyond further teaching, beyond changes in habits and skills. Helpers simply persevere. When they no longer have truths to tell, they can continue to "be true" to the patient and the patient's family. Such being true to another is fidelity beyond words. Humanly considered, both our fidelity through words and our fidelity beyond words reach their limits. But Scripture offers us some consolation, even when trouble brings us to the limit of our powers and stills the tongue: "The Spirit intercedes for us with sighs too deep for words."

The Organizational Mark and the Virtue of Public-Spiritedness

The disposition to organize can be traced back to the medieval guild and, still further back, to the Hippocratic covenant between the young physician and the teacher who helped initiate him into his professional identity. Following this tradition, Abraham Flexner believed that physicians should organize in order to maintain and improve professional standards. He maintained that a professional guild should differ from a trade association by aiming at self-improvement rather than self-promotion. So goes the ideal.

Until recently in the United States, it appeared that the organizational mark had all but faded, except for purely defensive and self-promotional activities upon the part of the guilds. The medical profession refined the general American myth of the self-made man into the myth of the freelance physician who ran his own office, made the rounds of his patients at their homes, and managed a practice partly by cash and partly by charity. But since the 1930s, medicine has increasingly organized to produce medical results in the setting of large hospitals and to expect compensation for the distribution of these goods and services through huge third-party payers. (The professional guild, like trade organizations, has been much less disposed to accept responsibility for controlling the quality of medical goods through the mechanism of self-regulation and discipline.)

This organizational mark calls for the professional virtue of "public-spiritedness," which I would define as the art of acting in concert with others for the common good in the production, distribution, and quality control of health care.

1. Public-Spiritedness and the Production of Medical Goods

In professing a body of knowledge that they place at the service of human need, physicians do perform in a purely private fashion. Medicine today is increasingly a social art practiced by a health care team in the setting of a very large institution. Until recently, the hospital served as the physician's workshop, where he or she performed services and made money under a third-party payment system with few controls over either those services or the money to be made. However, hospitals now operate under the restriction of a federal payment system that controls the amount of money the hospital (and, indirectly, the doctor) can make off a given disease and also under growing pressures from insurance companies and corporations negotiating health care contracts. Physicians must increasingly accept some responsibility not only for their personal professional values but also for the values shaping the institution in which they work. In effect, physicians need to recognize the hospital as a *polis,* a political entity, in which they must help set policies that weigh the ends served and the resources deployed to reach those ends. The ill require for their healing not only covenanted individuals but covenanted institutions that profess, testify on behalf of, or stand for something. Such institutions, in turn, need physicians skilled not simply in the art of medicine but also in the art of acting in concert with others for the common good.

Physicians need the virtue of public-spiritedness for the further reason that, whether in the hospital, the clinic, or in group practice, they are much less likely to work as solitary gunslingers than as members of a health care team. Medical education and residency training programs have only partly recognized the importance of preparing the professional to work as a member and leader of a health care team. They concentrate exhaustively and almost exclusively on educating students in the sciences and developing their technical skills, while paying much less attention to their maturation as team members.

Further, the very conditions of residency training often preclude effective teamwork. The constantly changing cast of specialists, attending physicians, residents, and nurses often leaves patients and their families wondering just who is their physician. The system also can signal to the impressionable resident that team membership is incidental and subordinate to technical performance. The ever-changing composition of the team, as shifts rotate, makes it difficult to deliver continuous, coherent service to a particular patient, however conscientious the team members. The accidental intersection of a variety of needed technical services does not spontaneously mesh into a coherent program of care. Clearly, the development of an effective team requires not only self-conscious efforts to prepare young members for participation and leadership but also the rethinking of training so as to honor the team's unitary responsibilities.

2. Public-Spiritedness and the
Distribution of Medical Goods

The notion of the just and public-spirited professional involves more than a minimalist commitment to what the moral tradition has called *commutative* justice (i.e., the fulfillment of duties between two private parties based on contracts). Public-spiritedness suggests a more spacious obligation to *distributive* justice that seeks to meet the health care needs of all members of society, a goal that has not been, and cannot be, met solely through the mechanism of the marketplace, the contract, and the supplements of charity. Physicians and other professionals have a duty to distribute goods and services to fulfill basic needs without limiting those services solely to those who have the capacity to pay for them. Some would deny this covenantal obligation to distributive justice altogether. Others would argue that the services of the helping professions should be distributed to meet such basic human needs but that this obligation rests on the society at large and not on the profession itself. This approach, which argues for a tax-supported third-party payment system, would eliminate *pro bono publico* work as a professional obligation.

Still others, myself included, see the obligation to distribute professional services as both a public and a professional responsibility. Professionals exercise power through authority the public grants them. The power they wield and the goods they control have a public magnitude and scale. Although the state must accept the primary responsibility for *ministering* justice (an old term for distributive justice), professional groups, too, have a ministry, if you will, to perform. When only the state accepts responsibility for distributive justice, the general sense of obligation tends to diminish in the culture at large, and the social virtue upon which the impetus to share depends diminishes and loses the grounds for its renewal. Professionals particularly need to accept some responsibility for ministering justice to sustain that moral sensibility in the society at large. Otherwise, the idealistic motives that originally prompted the founding of institutions such as mental hospitals will peter out, and the institutions will deteriorate into custodial bins.

Further, such *pro bono publico* work does not merely serve the private happiness of those individuals who receive services; it eventually redounds to the common good and fosters public happiness. Those who receive help are not merely individuals but parts of a whole. And the whole, in so serving its parts, serves its own public flourishing; it rescues its citizens mired in their private distress and frees them for a more public life. In the absence of *pro bono publico* work, we signal, in effect, that our society recognizes only those people who can pay their way into the marketplace. To the degree that this occurs, our public life shrinks; it dwindles to those with the money to enter it. Public-spirited professionals not only relieve private distress but help preserve our common life, in a monetary culture, from a constant threat that it will perish.

3. Public-Spiritedness and Professional Self-Regulation and Discipline

Physicians need the virtue of public-spiritedness not only to perform satisfactorily in health care teams in hospitals and to distribute the good of health care widely but also to control the quality of the care produced and distributed. Professional self-regulation and discipline ensure quality control.

For many reasons, physicians and their guilds avoid responsibility for professional self-monitoring. Like any professional group, they find themselves interlocked in personal relations with fellow professionals that make them reluctant to pursue disciplinary actions against one another or to champion the cause of abused patients against one another. And the stakes tend to be higher. Compared to lapses on the part of other professionals, the physician's therapeutic misadventures can more easily be fatal or irreparably harmful. The incompetent teacher merely bores his students to death, but the incompetent doctor can kill. Since the stakes are so high in the case of a physician's malpractice, professionals are tempted to draw their wagons into a circle to protect a challenged member. In general, Americans balk at pressing charges against their neighbors or colleagues; they dislike officiousness. Unlike some of their European counterparts, Americans show little stomach for playing amateur policeman, prosecutor, or judge when they themselves are not directly or officially involved in an incident. In many respects, this laissez-faire attitude is an admirable trait in the American character.

Yet this morally attractive nonchalance cannot justify permissiveness in professional life, for professionals often wield substantial power over persons who cannot judge their competence. They reserve the right to pass judgment (in professional matters) on colleagues or would-be colleagues, and the society supports this right by establishing educational requirements and licensing procedures. To be sure, patients profit from higher educational standards, but professionals also profit — substantially — in money and power. Professionals cannot justify this state-created monopoly if they merely practice competently themselves. "The individual's license to practice derives ultimately from the prior license to license," which the state has for all intents and purposes bestowed upon the guild. "If the license to practice carries with it the obligation to practice well, then the prior license to license carries with it the obligation to judge and monitor well."[12] Not only individuals but a guild must be accountable. Am I my colleague's keeper? The brief answer is yes. And that responsibility may sometimes require not simply disciplining the troubled colleague but also finding positive ways to help him. Public-spiritedness in this always-disturbing ac-

12. May, *The Physician's Covenant*, p. 134.

tivity of professional discipline calls for the attendant virtues of courage, fairness, and compassion.

The Original Source of Professing and the Virtue of Gratitude

Although the biblical covenant includes the four covenantal elements of gift, promise, and moral and ritual action, the discussion so far of the virtues has highlighted only the element of promise. The physician promises to profess his or her art (discerning knowledge) on behalf of someone (fidelity). We need now to make explicit the element of gift that precedes and generates the resources for this double promise to do something on behalf of someone. Otherwise, we interpret the professional either contractually as the seller of services or contractually/philanthropically as a combined seller/giver of services but not covenantally as a person whose actions rest upon a comprehensive receiving. We interpret the physician as benefactor but overlook his or her deepest identity as a beneficiary. Thereby we fail to trace the three covenantal virtues to their original source and their final resource, from which the virtues of gratitude and hope spring.

One cannot fully appreciate the indebtedness of a human being by toting up the varying sacrifices and investments made by others from which he or she benefits. The sense that one inexhaustibly receives presupposes an infinite inexhaustible source rather than the finite sum of discrete gifts received from others. Josef Pieper's formula — "Being precedes Truth and . . . Truth precedes Goodness" — neatly captures the element of infinite gift upon which the virtues depend. Knowing depends upon the taking in of Being (Being precedes Truth), and goodness (or doing right) depends upon that receptive knowing (Truth precedes Goodness). In the biblical tradition, this transcendent source is a Being which is a Being-true that, in covenant fidelity, suffuses to every authentic gift between human beings. The secondary gifts in the human order of giving and receiving can only (and imperfectly) signify this primary gift.

But gifts received at the human level also contribute to the physician's knowing and doing. No one can graduate from a modern university and professional school and think of himself or herself as a self-made man or woman. Practicing physicians cannot survive a single day without drawing upon the massive research that supports whatever prowess is theirs in diagnosis, prognosis, and therapy. Not only past generations of researchers but countless patients, most of them poor, have submitted to the experiments that now make the physician seem so smart in the office, the clinic, or the hospital. Further, that research tradition does not, in practice, connect (in the office or clinic) with the individual patient unless the patient himself presents, complains, lays bare his vulnerability and distress. The successful interview is a two-way exchange of giving and receiving. The physician must talk but also listen; the interview requires the tongue but also the ear.

Thus, professionals who, in fidelity, benefit their patients do not do so as pure benefactors. Idealistic members of the helping professions like to define themselves solely in terms of their giving or serving — thus putting others in debt to them. A reciprocity, however, of giving and receiving is at work in the professional relationship. The physician has received abundantly from her patients, not only in all the aforementioned ways but also by their petitions for help, which confer upon the physician her identity. Patients help give the professional her calling. In answering the call, the professional gets back nothing less than what she is becoming — a remarkable gift indeed.

Final Resource and the Virtue of Hope

In trying to make good on their calling, professionals discover that they fall short. They promise a deep-going, core identification with their patients but discover that they risk getting mired in the mess and confusion of their patients' lives. Drawing close to misery and deprivation threatens to suck them down into a whirlpool. Some physicians respond to human affliction heroically and grimly, acting the part of savior, the anointed defender and guardian of the woebeset. Others, discouraged, recognize the very limited, partial, and temporary nature of the relief they can offer, and they burn out. Still others respond self-protectively, finding a way to shield themselves defensively from the stricken, radioactive patient. While differing, these three responses share a metaphysical gloom; they raise the question of the place of the virtue of hope in the helping professions.

The response of the grim saviors (the Dr. Kevorkians) fails to honor the limits of professional power. Defining a professor exclusively in terms of a contractual fight against a negative — the fight against suffering and death — eventually begins to impose all sorts of negatives upon the patient in the name of the unconditional battle. Wars against the negative tend to become total and acquire an imperial momentum and force. We have seen this in the world of politics. The demagogue identifies and demonizes the mortal enemy of the people and then justifies practices and restrictions on liberty in order to defeat that enemy. So also in the professions. The fight against suffering and death should not supply medicine with its controlling unconditional aim. The active euthanasia movement surfaced as a reaction against an unconditional fight against death that gratuitously imposed suffering upon patients. But in its care of the dying, which seeks to eliminate altogether the patient's suffering, it in turn exposes society to secondary impacts of the sort detailed in the first chapter of this book. Dan Callahan wisely suggested that

"Medicine should try to relieve human suffering, but only that suffering which is brought on by illness and dying as biological phenomena, not that suffering which comes from anguish or despair at the human condition."[13]

In the same vein, Stephen Post has asserted that "Euthanasia and Assisted Suicide are conceptually flawed if the motive underlying them is the elimination of suffering."[14] Suffering is not simply an evil on a continuum such that we can rightly say that the more we can reduce it, the better — and best of all if we can eliminate it completely. Trying to eliminate suffering differs essentially from modestly trying to reduce it. The eliminator shifts into a messianic mode. The total controller is out of control. The difficulties in sustaining that messianic role cause some practitioners to burn out and others to act simply to protect themselves in a sea of misery.

A covenantal ethic does not inspire hope if it merely generates a moral principle of unconditional fidelity and nothing more. Indeed, as a moral principle alone, unconditional fidelity only intensifies professional burdens and increases the possibility of moral exhaustion and burnout. A covenantal ethic depends upon the conviction that one's own promise-keeping rests not simply on a moral principle of keeping one's promises but upon an all-surrounding promissory event. God has made and will keep his promises to humankind. This promise defines men and women not only retrospectively in gratitude but prospectively in hope. It comforts them in the midst of their professional excesses, shortfalls, and burnouts with the knowledge that God will not abandon his creatures, either those

13. Callahan, "When Self-Determination Runs Amok," *Hastings Center Report* 22 (March-April 1992): 55.

14. Post, "American Culture and Euthanasia," *Health Progress,* December 1991, p. 37. Professor Post goes on to say, "The desire to control pain has always been valid, but not the desire to press control so far as to directly cause death, itself. Death by lethal injection is best understood as a tyranny of technological control" (p. 37).

who give care or those who receive it. God's promise gives to human promise-keeping some buoyancy. To the degree that professionals persist in "being true" to their promises, even with only a small measure of resiliency, they offer their troubled patients a tiny emblem of that ultimate hope.

The Limits of the Medical Covenant:
Medical Futility

The concept of "medical futility" has emerged in the middle 1990s as a way of placing a limit on the physician's and the health care organization's medical covenant with a gravely ill patient. The term refers to a set of variously defined conditions under which it can appropriately be concluded that further medical treatment of a patient would be futile, thereby relieving the health care practitioner and the delivery system of any obligation to provide additional treatment. The concept has proved especially attractive to some interested parties as we increasingly move from a fee-for-service to a prepayment health care system, which introduces financial incentives for the health care organization, and often the doctor, to limit the cost of services rendered to individual patients. The provider receives fixed annual prepayments from patients and therefore suffers financially to the degree health care costs for individual patients exceed that prepayment. A verdict of "medical futility" would, in some cases, free providers from having to provide costly services. The following case poses some of the issues that we face in determining the legitimate limits to medical care.

A two-year-old child nearly drowns in her parents' swimming pool, from which she is pulled, lifeless, after having been submerged for approximately thirty minutes. A lengthy resuscitation results in severe acidosis and a very low oxygen level. While doctors stabilize her cardiovascular function and note some (apart from spinal cord) reflexes and spontaneous movement, her EEG (nearly flat) and her neurological exam are very abnormal. Her breathing is being sustained only by mechanical ventilation, and she is receiving intravenous fluids and nutrition. The physicians have very high confidence in a very low level of neurological function *if* she survives. Her parents elect to withdraw care.

There are two ways of approaching the case of this child, woefully damaged (nearly flat EEG) and almost dead after spending thirty minutes submerged in water. The first approach would narrowly define (and resolve) the question of treatment by resort to general standards of medical futility. Lawrence J. Schneiderman (M.D.), Nancy S. Jecker (Ph.D.), and Albert R. Jonsen (Ph.D.) have proposed a representative set of such standards, both quantitative and qualitative, in an article entitled "Medical Futility: Its Meaning and Ethical Implications." They call on the physician to consider both the likelihood and the quality of an outcome before making a determination of medical futility.

Among the quantitative guidelines, they specify that physicians should regard a treatment as futile only when they "conclude (either through personal experience, experiences shared with colleagues, or consideration of reported empiric data) that in the last 100 cases, a medical treatment has been useless."[1] They contend that the extremely rare success should not of itself weaken the quantitative judgment that a procedure is futile. The possibility of a so-called "miracle" should not tyrannize in decision-making.

Among the qualitative guidelines, Schneiderman and his col-

---

1. Schneiderman, Jecker, and Jonsen, "Medical Futility: Its Meaning and Ethical Implications," *Annals of Internal Medicine* 112 (1990): 951.

leagues state that a treatment is futile if it merely preserves the patient in a state of "permanent unconsciousness or cannot end dependence on intensive medical care."[2] In other words, the utility of a treatment depends upon its producing not just an *effect* (almost all medical procedures will produce some kind of effect) but a *benefit* for the patient. The procedure that merely produces a persistent vegetative state hardly benefits the patient. Neither does the treatment that leaves the patient wholly preoccupied and submerged in intensive care utterly unable to achieve any other goals in life.

As a practical matter, the establishment of general qualitative guidelines will typically lead to the establishment of quantitative guidelines. In treating newborns, for example, one might rely on certain numerical markers for determining not only whether the infant will survive but what the likely quality of that survival will be. For example, one might agree to five hundred grams' weight and twenty-five weeks' gestation as the dividing line below which one has only the duty to give comfort care and above which the additional duty to rescue comes into play.

According to proponents of the concept of medical futility, unless a treatment satisfies both quantitative and qualitative standards, physicians are entitled (in concert with other health care professionals *but without the consent of either patients or their families*) to withhold treatment. Accordingly, by one set of established standards, the two-year-old submerged in water for approximately thirty minutes would not qualify for medical treatment. While treatment might satisfy the quantitative standard *as directed to the limited goal of ensuring the child's biological survival,* it would fail qualitatively. At best, the child would survive in a persistent vegetable state, wholly dependent upon overwhelming medical assists. She would lack both the capacity and the opportunity for pursuing any goals in life. And so the child's doctors would have no duty to treat.

2. Schneiderman, Jecker, and Jonsen, "Medical Futility," p. 949.

In the case cited, the parents elected to withdraw treatment. But let us suppose that they had disagreed about withdrawing life supports — or, more daunting still, that they had requested/demanded that everything be done for their child. According to Schneiderman and his colleagues, the doctors would still have been entitled to withhold treatment.

There are six ways of interpreting this bestowal of exclusive power upon doctors to withhold treatment: (1) as an affirmation of professional autonomy, (2) as a defense of professional integrity, (3) as a parentalistic exercise of professional power, (4) as a protection of the interests of third parties, (5) as an advance of the interests of a second party (the physician or the provider), and (6) as a too-limited understanding of the physician's responsibility to the patient and the patient's family.

1. An Affirmation of Professional Autonomy

Some endorse the doctor's exercise of unilateral power in withholding futile treatment as affirming the physician's autonomy. Writing in the *Journal of Law and Medicine,* Judith F. Daar frames the issue in those terms in the very title of her article "Medical Futility and Implications for Physician Autonomy." Perhaps linking the notion of medical futility with the question of the physician's autonomy is inevitable in legal contexts. In ruling on such disputes between patients and physicians, courts have had to determine where the power of making decisions lies, and in doing so they have often relied on rights language.

As Daar points out, the courts have generally vested the right to make decisions about possible medical benefits in patients (or in their surrogates when the patients themselves are incompetent) rather than in their doctors. For example, the courts found in favor of family members in the cases of the eighty-five-year-old Minnesotan Helen Wanglie, who persisted in a vegetative state, unable to breathe or eat on her own, and Baby K, an anencephalic infant in Virginia who periodically needed emergency respiratory support.[3] In both cases, when physicians petitioned the courts to let them refuse treatment, the physicians suffered a curtailment of their autonomy, their right to make decisions. The disposition of the cases rendered "physicians more susceptible to legal, rather than medical judgments about the provision of care."[4]

2. A Defense of Professional Integrity

Some endorse the bestowal of unilateral power on physicians to withhold treatment on grounds of medical futility not in affirmation of abstract autonomy but in defense of professional integrity. They contend that the negative right of autonomy — the right to be free from the interference of patients, families, and the courts in determining medical futility — rests upon the positive medical duty to treat coherently. Futile treatment collapses into medical incoherence, they argue; thus, in order to preserve the integrity, the wholeness, if you will, of a given medical performance, physicians must retain the right to refuse to treat. Patients and their families look to the medical community for a benefit beyond their own capacity to effect, but patients and families should not be allowed to demand that a doctor perform an action that is inherently futile either in the sense that the effect cannot be attained or that the effect attained is not a medical benefit. A professional professes something (a body of knowledge) on behalf of someone (the patient and his or her family). What the professional professes constrains what the patient

3. Daar, "Medical Futility and Implications for Physician Autonomy," *American Journal of Law and Medicine* 21 (1995): 223-29.
4. Daar, "Medical Futility and Implications for Physician Autonomy," p. 229.

or surrogate can ask for. The obligation to profess a body of knowledge "on behalf of" does not convert into a requirement that one act "under the orders of." The professing act cannot cut its tie with the content of what is professed without losing its integrity.

3. A Parentalistic Exercise of Professional Power

Some critics maintain that when doctors seek to determine medical futility unilaterally, they are engaging in an unjustifiable parentalistic exercise of power. Such critics concede that physicians may be in the best position to judge what effects a medical procedure will produce, but they insist that patients and families should be allowed to determine whether that effect (e.g., bare survival in a persistent vegetative state) offers a benefit. They contend that professionals reach beyond a medical judgment and usurp the power of the patient and the patient's family when they insist that they alone have the right to make that decision. Thus Robert Veatch, the ever-vigilant antiparentalist, would have us accede to the values and judgment of the patient or the family, not the doctor, in determining futility qualitatively.[5] The beneficiaries, not the benefactor, should be allowed to judge whether the result of biological existence is a benefit rather than a nullity or worse.

4. Protection of Third-Party Interests

Some contend that doctors should be empowered to withhold treatments that are either futile or marginally useful in order to protect

5. See Robert M. Veatch and Carol Mason Spicer, "Medical Futility Care: The Role of the Physician in Setting Limits," *American Journal of Law and Medicine* 15 (1992): 18.

the interests of third parties — principally other claimants upon the use of finite resources. For example, some have argued that, given the limited number of donors available for heart transplant operations, such procedures should be denied to smokers with other associated systemic ailments in favor of patients who have maintained comparatively healthier lifestyles.[6] This constitutes much shakier ground for an argument in favor of a doctor's right to exercise unilateral power in withholding futile treatment than the three preceding views do, however. If physicians are to withhold treatment, they must do so because the proposed treatment fails to offer a benefit, not because it offers less benefit than an alternative use of time and resources. Were they to make such treatment determinations on the basis of third-party interests, physicians and provider organizations would be violating their covenant with the patient in order to act as the administrator/judge of competing claims.

5. Promotion of Second-Party Interests

There is a clear danger that the notion of medical futility could be abused simply to protect the financial interests of the second party to the medical covenant, the physician or the provider organization. A physician's chief obligation is to treat for the benefit of a patient, not to withhold treatment because it serves either his or her own financial interests or the bottom line of the provider organization from whose profits he or she may derivatively benefit. Interestingly enough, the courts have not ruled against such abuse on the part of physicians or provider organizations if in their contracts with patients they have stated clearly what they will and will not do. In

6. It should be noted that Schneiderman, Jecker, and Jonsen do not resort to this argument. "Our notion of futility does not arise from consideration of scarce resources" ("Medical Futility," p. 953).

the case of the two-year-old child in the pool, in order to avoid legal obligation to treat, the provider organization would only have had to specify in its contract with the family that it would not cover treatment that will produce only a chronic vegetative state. If reimbursement for a treatment is clearly excluded in a contract, whether medically appropriate or not, the provider is under no legal obligation to provide it. In effect, the issue of medical utility/futility yields to the purely commercial contractual issue of whether a given service is covered.

Further, the burden of initiative and proof in such contractual disputes shifts from doctors, where it lay in the Wanglie and the Baby K cases, to patients, where it lay in *Goepel v. Mail Handlers Benefit Plan* and *Barnett v. Kaiser Foundation Health Plan*.[7] In the former set of cases, the doctors had to take the initiative in seeking permission to refuse treatment; in the latter set, patients/families had to go to court to pursue a reversal of a provider organization's interpretation of its own contracts. Patient/family autonomy yielded in the latter cases not to the ideals of professional integrity or parentalism but to the marketplace ethics of the contract. Where reimbursement for a treatment was excluded in a contract, whether medically appropriate or not, the provider was found to be under no obligation to provide it. This restriction of accountability to the terms of the contract washes out not only the distinction between futility and utility but also the larger notion of professional responsibility, insofar as it denies that professionals have any obligation to profess something on behalf of someone else without regard to its financial consequences for themselves.

7. See Daar, "Medical Futility and Implications for Physician Autonomy," pp. 236-39.

6. A Too-Limited Understanding of the Physician's Responsibility to the Patient and the Patient's Family

Finally, some have criticized efforts to grant doctors exclusive power to withhold treatment on the grounds that this power does not adequately honor the full range of the physician's responsibility for her patients and their families. To understand this criticism, we must further explore the assertion I made at the beginning of this chapter that the attempt to establish general standards of medical practices — in this case, concerning futile treatment — supplies us with only one of two basic approaches to medical ethics.

So far, we have been pursuing what might generally be called a rights-based approach to the case. Rights-oriented thinking begins with the natural capacities of an individual, such as intelligence or bare biological existence, abstracted from the historical accidents of family, religion, education, and the like, and seeks to determine what duties of care we owe to *all* human beings who possess and evidence these capacities. This approach, applied to intensive care for the young, has led to an effort to establish general standards and guidelines. For example, with respect to the newborn, it has led to markers of at least 500 grams in weight and at least 25 weeks of gestation as the dividing line below which one has no duty to rescue, only the duty to give comfort care, and above which the additional duty to rescue comes into play.

This rights-based approach to cases leads to a natural overlapping of ethics with the law. Ethics so understood operates, like the law, at a level of generality and universality. One thinks of the rights that all members of a class enjoy, irrespective of the accidents of hair color, race, family, and the like. Similarly, the law, to be the law, must be universal — that is, no respecter of persons. Both rights language and legal language seek out the universal to define moral duties and to enact and perhaps to enforce laws that embody those rights. Thus the law and ethics overlap.

Why, then, in cases involving the newborn and young, for which some general guidelines have been established, must we still pay serious attention to the parents' wishes in disputes over treatment? Here moral language more relational and role-defined comes into play. Such language does not affix value to a life according to impersonal standards, abstracted from all particular ties, but recognizes the power and valency of bonding in human life. Such language justifies our customary sensitivity to parental authority.

Bonding is the tie that binds in human life. Offspring of the lower primates cling to the bodies of their mothers; marsupials hang on for dear life. But the human infant is unable to cling. A mother must actively cradle her child, tend to it, cherish it for it fully to flourish. Bonding engenders loyalty to the being and well-being of another. In a sense, *loyalty* is too weak a term, since it suggests a relation that depends upon the will of both parties. Bonding is a matter of two people settling into one another's bone marrow and kidneys, imagination and bowels. Bonding establishes a tie so powerful that neither can undertake much without reckoning with the consequences for the being and well-being of the other. Bonding is the reality in the natural order that covenants crown and seal.

On the whole we have adopted approaches to decision making that value the relationship between human beings for its clues to their being and value and our obligations to them rather than simply assigning values according to the numbers scored on tests and traced on charts. Thus normally and usually we defer to parents in decisions of great moment for their infants and children.

The approach advocated by Schneiderman and his colleagues of unilaterally withholding treatment obtusely neglects the power of bonding between parents and children. In letting go of a child, parents must let go of a part of themselves. Indeed, they would gladly surrender a part of themselves if they thought that action would secure the well-being of the child. Whatever happens, they will not come out of this grievous event the same persons. Their being, their way of being in the world, suffers a profound alteration.

Physicians, if they would be healers, cannot focus narrowly on the question of medical futility and proceed from that judgment to the next case. The judgment that treatment is futile does not mean that the effort to heal is futile. And the work of healing has hardly begun when the full import of the disaster strikes home to the parents, their child's lifeless body having just been pulled from the pool. In the case cited, the parents apparently needed no time to reach a decision not to treat, but many parents would, and the power of bonding ought to prevent doctors from too quickly taking refuge in the judgment of medical futility and thus diminishing the full measure of the professional bond that binds them to the parents-bonded-to-the-child. They will need to help the parents work through the terrible mutilation that their own lives will undergo. And, even in the case of the parents who have quickly agreed to the letting go, one must not underestimate the turbulent times that they face ahead — particularly in this case, a drowning in a swimming pool, perhaps a pool that the parents chose to put in or that served as a chief attraction of the house they chose to buy or rent. The proviso that permits a unilateral judgment of medical futility but does not require the physicians to work through the decision with patients is less a parentalist usurpation of power than a diminution of responsibility.

I am not arguing here for an uncritical deference to parental wishes or suggesting that a society cannot set limits to the treatments it will pay for. However, we too narrowly define the professional's responsibility in the midst of the family's tribulation if we reduce the responsibility to the choice of either treating or withdrawing treatment. That choice is but a fraction of the total responsibility of caregivers.

In hard decisions, such as pulling the plug, parents face two decisions: (1) the original decision of whether or not to withdraw treatment and (2) the decision (i.e., the firm resolution) to make good on the original decision. Since, in a hard decision, parents will face a turbulent passage no matter which way they (or others) decide, their caregivers dare not, in their rush to judgment on the first decision, fail to honor the importance of the second decision, especially for parents, who, above all others, must live with the consequences of the original decision.

The Schneiderman article does not entirely ignore the parents' stake in the decision and outcome. It admits of exceptions, and it cautions against peremptory unilateral action in at least some cases. While asserting that "futility is a professional judgment that . . . permits physicians to withhold or withdraw treatment deemed to be inappropriate without subjecting such a decision to patient approval," the authors concede that on "compassionate grounds" physicians may decide to keep a patient alive long enough, for example, "to see a son or a daughter not yet arrived" or "to facilitate coping and grieving by family members."[8] But the language surrounding the exceptions is somewhat dismissive and condescending. The authors refer to the "emotional bias" and "emotional investments" of others — phrases that but palely reflect the power of bonding in human life. The phrases imply that the physician occupies a higher, more distanced rational ground that justifies withdrawing treatment unilaterally and forthwith, except for a compassionate accommodation to a biased — that is, irrational — state of affairs. But parents are *bonded* to their children, not just emotionally invested in them. And some would see in the power of bonding — conjugal, parental, filial, fraternal, sororal, compassionate, and even professional — one of the defining marks of our humanity that it would be irrational to marginalize by treating medical futility simply as a matter of drawing lines between the rights of two competing sources of autonomous power.

8. Schneiderman, Jecker, and Jonsen, "Medical Futility," p. 953.

I do not want to overstate the contrast between the two types of moral language, one emphasizing and the other abstracting from human ties. Bonding, after all, requires some minimal level of percipience on both sides to be sustained over time. Thus one can argue that a relational understanding of human life itself argues for the setting of guidelines seemingly impersonal and abstracted from particular ties.

Further, a relational understanding of human selves and their flourishing provides grounds for buttressing their rights — that is, their claims against those who violate relational responsibilities of care, including parents, professionals, teachers, and others. Moreover, a relational approach cannot seriously claim to derive notions of worth, rights, and duties solely from the testimony of those who bond to one another. If worth and rights depend upon a human tie alone, the less powerful member of a pair — the retarded child, the impaired infant, the battered spouse — would be wholly hostage to the erratic valuations and decisions of parents, mates, and caregivers, good, bad, or indifferent. That is why moralists have tried to establish the notion of worth irrespective of ties. Their minimalism sought to prevent worse fates. The battered child silences foolish sentimentality about the successful rate of bonding. Parents cannot claim to be the sole or final arbiters of the value and rights of their children. Frail themselves, and facing a process of bonding often strewn with obstacles, parents do not always bond wisely and well. This consideration justifies the professional's and the state's duty to protect children from abusive parents, to appoint other guardians in their place, and to expect from these guardians a conscientious discharge of their substituted parental role. It also forbids doctors from simply indulging the most extravagant of medical demands from patients and families. Some parents bond too zealously to their children, to the exclusion of all other commitments and covenants. That is why the biblical tradition looks to God's more comprehensive covenant with all creatures as the measure and standard for the several covenants in and through which we keep faith with one another. In brief, we limit the doctor's alternatives too much if we narrow them to unilateral decision making on the one hand and submissive, technical facilitating on the other. Most care for critically ill children and their families requires not recipe books for action but a cultivation of the virtues of discernment and fidelity, which those who profess something on behalf of someone must evince if they would practice not perfectly but well.

Keeping Covenant and
Health Care Reform

The discrete policy issue of active/passive euthanasia inevitably poses questions about the health care system and the kind of coverage it offers. For example, the U.S. health care system provides neither universal nor comprehensive coverage. These shortcomings of the system bear directly on several of the arguments for passive and active euthanasia. In the absence of a system that reaches all sick people, campaigns calling for *voluntary* euthanasia ring false. Voluntariness of choice presupposes alternatives. When acute care fails to reach many people and offer alternatives, their choice of active euthanasia is hardly uncoerced. Abandonment pushes them toward euthanasia, and abandonment wholly prevents them from choosing passive euthanasia. A system that denies them treatment cannot smugly claim that it merely allows them to die; it consigns them to death and hardly with mercy.

Further, in order to claim compassion as a motive in either killing or allowing to die, a system must provide not only universal but comprehensive coverage. A health care system that supplies universal acute-care coverage but does not follow through comprehensively with rehabilitative, long-term, and terminal care rescues some patients from death only to impose upon them the catastrophe of continuing life without adequate care. Many massively damaged

99

patients would rather die than survive bereft of support or fated to impose an unendurable and unmitigated burden on an aged mate. Thus discussion of the discrete policy issue of active/passive euthanasia quickly broadens out into inquiry about the scope and contours of the health care system.

However, a credible exploration of a subject as complex as health care reform cannot simply supply arguments about the limited subject of active/passive euthanasia. Accordingly, I will not try to bend every comment on the health care system to that limited policy issue alone. Still, the increased prominence of both issues in the 1990s is not accidental. Omissions and distortions in the health care system can increase pressures for active euthanasia as well as undercut the integrity of arguments for passive euthanasia.

The Problem

Our health care system contains much of which we should be proud and much that we should conserve. It has enlisted the devotion of millions of health care professionals, created splendid hospitals, clinics, and research institutions, and dazzled the world with its technical achievements. And it has allowed for some choice in doctors. Any reform of the system must preserve its virtues.

Yet our health care system is seriously flawed. It fails to reach many of us: at any given time, it excludes over one out of seven Americans (about forty million people) from health care insurance; it leaves another one out of seven underinsured. The consequences for individuals and families are devastating. When we exclude people from health care, they suffer a triple deprivation — the pain of illness, the desperation of little or no treatment, and the cruel proof that they do not really belong to the community. We make them strangers and sojourners in their own land.

When we do not care, we also diminish the vigor of our common life. Sick people cannot work productively. In relieving individual, private distress, a nation enables its people to contribute more fully to public life and to economic well-being. Thereby the nation serves its own public flourishing, not only instrumentally but also morally and psychologically to the degree that it signals by its care the strength of its covenant with its own.

Our system also does not offer enough primary, preventive, home, and long-term care, and it woefully neglects mental health coverage. We tend to be acute-care gluttons and preventive-care anemics.

Reflecting this lopsided emphasis on acute care, the system over-supplies us with specialists (some 70 percent of our doctors are specialists, compared with only 30 to 50 percent in other industrial countries) and undersupplies us with generalists, whom we need for effective preventive, rehabilitative, and long-term care.

The system pays for procedures contracted for and performed rather than good health outcomes achieved and exposes those who cannot pay to dramatically lower success rates for a given procedure. It often overtreats; yet insurance sometimes deserts when most needed. It exposes people who have lost their jobs to financial ruin. It locks others with preexisting conditions into jobs they do not want. And the system often establishes lifetime limits on care.

The system burdens health care practitioners and institutions with too many regulations and forms. A financial officer at one hospital reports that her staff has to handle some 3,200 different types of accounts receivable. The head of the major city hospital in Dallas says that he needs a staff of three hundred people to handle what, at a comparable hospital under the Canadian system, three people dispatch handily.

Our system also costs more to operate than any other health care system in the world. No other country spends more than 10 percent of its gross domestic product for health care, yet we are currently above 14 percent, and if we maintain the current level of care, costs will rise still further. The system now consumes one-seventh of everything that we make or do. Even this figure does not fully measure the cost. The "fringe benefit" of health care is anything but a fringe cost of producing cars, computers, refrigerators, and, for that matter, education. In some of our industries, health benefits cost more than anything except wages and salaries. This cost reduces the competitiveness of businesses in the United States. Why should companies build cars in Detroit if their health care costs per worker are $500 to $750 lower across the bridge in Windsor, Canada? Some commentators have argued that we have recently slowed down the increasing costs of medical care. But under three presidents we have undergone temporary slowdowns in costs only to see them speed up again. For our own sake and the sake of our children, we must be better stewards of our nation's resources.

Further, our payment system is unfair. Businesses, insurance companies, hospitals, the government, and patients furiously shift costs as they fob off their expenses on others. Hospitals jack up their prices to the insured to cover their costs in caring for indigent patients. Some doctors try to skim off well-insured patients while rejecting others. Insurance companies try to pick healthy customers and evade payouts to the sick. Companies shift to part-time, temporary, or younger employees to reduce health insurance costs. The government's savings on Medicare and Medicaid patients sometimes come at the expense of prices paid by insured patients. Some people are forced to stay on welfare because low-paying jobs in service industries do not provide the health insurance they receive under Medicaid. All this artful dodging eventually dumps costs on workers and taxpayers through lower salary raises, higher taxes, and higher insurance payments.

Ethical Foundations

A major reform of our health care system would rank as the most comprehensive piece of social legislation since the establishment of

our Social Security system. We cannot engage in so grand an un-
dertaking without being clear about its moral foundations. In my
judgment, those foundations are three: *health care is a fundamental
good; health care is not the only fundamental good;* and *health care is
a public good.*

1. A Fundamental Good

Health care is a fundamental good because it is one of the necessities
of life. It is not an optional commodity, like a Walkman, a tie, or
a scarf. Mothers instinctively affirm this truth when they concentrate
their hopes on just this: the birth of a healthy baby — ten fingers,
ten toes, a good heart, robust lungs. Why this single, humble,
anxious wish? The mother prizes her baby's health because of the
promise it holds for the child's life and flourishing. Healthy children,
and therefore health care, are part of a nation's covenant with its
future.

Because health care is a fundamental good, the American system
must honor and reflect the following moral principles.

The system must offer universal access. Health benefits should reach
all of us without financial or other barriers. Citizens should not fear
that part-time or temporary employment or a change or loss of a
job will cost them their health care. No one should lose access to
health insurance because of preexisting conditions, age, race, or
genetic background. Barriers to access arising from linguistic and
cultural differences, geographical distance, and disability must also
come down.

Why should Americans especially insist that a basic good, such
as health care, ought to reach all citizens? Our three major religious
traditions — Protestant, Catholic, and Jewish — are communitarian. They all insist that we leave no one out in the cold when naked,
starved, or sick.

Some individualists may counter that our revolutionary emphasis on individual liberty broke with this communitarian heritage. This view of our past, however, overlooks the first words we spoke as a nation: "We, the people." The preamble to the Constitution does not proclaim "We, the factions of the United States" or "We, the interest groups of the United States" or "We, the individuals of the United States" but "We, the people." That declaration was tested and affirmed through the bitter ordeal of the Civil War. We could not survive half slave, half free. Neither can we stand divided half sick and half well, half protected and half uninsured. Our flourishing as a people depends upon our ability to create a health care system that binds us together as a nation. The principle of universal access goes to the soul of reform. Currently, we are the only industrial nation other than South Africa that fails to offer universal access.

The system must be comprehensive. Benefits must meet the full range of health care needs. We should offer primary, preventive, and some long-term care as well as acute care, home as well as hospital care, and treatment for mental as well as physical illness. An observer once saw through our lopsided allocations in the U.S. when he wrote, "Our system's philosophy might be condensed in the motto, 'Millions for [acute] care and not one cent for prevention!'" Those lines were written in 1886. When we attend too little to primary, preventive, and mental health care, the cost of acute care increases, we mistarget funds, and we fail to help people take responsibility for their own health.

When we do not offer comprehensive coverage, we also fail to offer universal coverage. We discriminate against whole classes of the afflicted, such as the mentally ill and those in need of long-term care. We would consider it strange to propose treating renal disease but not heart disease, but many plans currently lavish care on the physically ill while ignoring the mentally ill. A scheme that aspires to universal coverage must offer a comprehensive package.

The system must be fair. It should not create a two-nation system

— dividing the nation or dividing the generations over this fundamental good. It should spread the costs and burdens of meeting our health care needs fairly, across the entire community.

Some might respond that the uninsured now receive the benefit of care through the emergency room. Unfortunately, the care they receive does not match the care the insured receive. Their mortality rate for a given procedure is 1.8 times higher than the rate for the insured. The astronomical costs of some acute and long-term services can impoverish the sick and disabled and their families, and it imperils the security of those of us who have not yet been stricken.

We would find it absurd to limit the protection afforded by the Defense Department — another fundamental good — to only those who can afford a private army. We ought not to limit access to medical care only to those who can hire a platoon of doctors.

We also need a system that fairly shares the cost of health care. We must secure contributions from all and eliminate the widespread patterns of cost shifting and freeloading. A fair sharing of benefits and burdens would draw the community together and tie the generations to one another.

The system must be of high quality. Health care is too important a good not to be good. Fostering good quality requires providing health care professionals with an environment that encourages their best work, protects the integrity of professional judgment, delivers effective treatments, and weeds out unethical and incompetent practitioners. It also requires providing patients with sufficient information about the outcomes achieved by different plans to help them make informed, rational choices.

Ordinarily, consumers in the marketplace can enforce quality through their ability to compare products knowledgeably. But patients today do not have the information to make those judgments about doctors, hospitals, and health care plans — and it is difficult to acquire this knowledge in the midst of a medical crisis. Without the assurance of quality in the basic health care package, the well-to-do will buy up and out, returning the country to a two-nation health care system.

Health care is also too important a good not to get better. Therefore, the system must also support research for improving the full range of health care services, including research on the outcomes of health care and more research directed to preventive, rehabilitative, and terminal care. We currently allocate almost all our research money to fight death, very little to ease pain and suffering for the living and dying.

The system must be responsive to choice. Health care is too fundamental a good, affecting each of us too intimately and fatefully, not to give us some measure of freedom to choose our doctors, the treatments we receive, and the health care plans in which we receive them. Too many people lack choice altogether or enjoy choice in only one of these areas. Honoring choice in the health care system not only respects liberty but also engages the patient in the activity of preventive, acute, rehabilitative, and long-term care.

2. Not the Only Fundamental Good

Health care is not the only fundamental good. We must also defend the nation, provide housing, and educate our children. Thus we need a system that allocates wisely and manages efficiently so that we can pay for these other basic goods.

To enable us to allocate wisely, the health care system must let us compare and balance what we spend on health care against other national priorities and evaluate and choose among diverse health services. Thus far, the structure and funding of the health care system has not given us enough information about costs to let us make clear choices among these priorities. We need this information to put ourselves in a better position to meet all our other social needs and also to decide more wisely among competing health care needs.

Efficient and cost-effective management is a moral, not just an economic, imperative. Ethics and economics are not wholly distinct spheres. The British universities were right when they linked the study of economics, politics, and philosophy. Ethics, politics, and economics interconnect.

The health care system should also be simple to use, free of bureaucratic roadblocks that hinder the delivery of care. I have two daughters who are physicians, and they find it discouraging when the person at the other end of that 800 line who has been empowered to approve or refuse a treatment routinely asks things like "How do you spell manic-depressive?" Sen. Robert Dole criticized the Clinton plan for its complexity by showing an organizational chart of the plan on TV: he did not mention that the current system is so complex that one could not even bring it into view on a TV camera. Nevertheless, Senator Dole had a point. Whatever the reform plan, it must offer simple access for patients and ease of management for doctors and other caregivers. The Clinton administration, sensitive to this need, sought to make provider organizations rather than a National Health Council or statewide purchasing alliances responsible for individual patient care.

A new system will also need to reduce administrative costs. Fifteen hundred insurance companies currently compete for our health care dollars, producing huge redundancies and complexities in administrative and advertising costs. Moreover, these companies largely compete not in matters of price and quality but in the arts of "cherry picking" customers who are less likely to fall sick or of designing benefits packages that limit the claims of those who do fall sick.

Efficiency must be defined with a wise heart, not just a calculator. Medical cookbooks should not bind providers; society should encourage them to adopt wise treatment guidelines. Inevitably, controlling costs involves setting priorities among health care needs and respecting distinctions between needs and wants, effectiveness and futility. Efficiency in the service of universal access is a virtue, not a constraint. It can offer choices and opportunities for health care for all people instead of denying choice to millions. We must allocate our resources wisely so that we can achieve the goals of our health care system and address our other national needs.

3. A Public Good

Health care is a public good. Thus a good system must help increase our sense of responsibility, both as providers and as consumers. A huge social investment has helped to educate health care professionals and sustain the good they offer. Federal outlays for research and medical education, patients who allow young residents to practice on their bodies as they learn their art, community chest drives, foundation gifts, corporate grants, municipal taxes, bonds floated to build hospitals — all these social supports refute the notion that health care is exclusively a private skill or a commodity up for grabs by the highest bidder. A society that recognizes and honors the social derivation of health care cannot plausibly reduce the distressed patient to a mere profit opportunity or to an object of hit-or-miss charity.

The indebtedness of professionals vastly exceeds the loans or fellowships they have received. Recognizing that they are not self-made, thousands of young professionals want to give back, even as they have received. The health care system must foster ways in which practitioners can make good on their profession as a calling, not just a job. The system must protect the integrity of professional judgment, weed out the incompetent or unethical practitioner, and encourage excellence.

The success of a health care system also depends upon an increased sense of responsibility on the part of patients. We cannot solve our problems through a social mechanism alone. The success or failure of a system depends upon the "habits of the heart" of a citizenry. Patients must be active partners in their health care. Preventing a heart attack, rehabilitating a spinal injury, coping with a stroke — these often require changes in a patient's habits. The system cannot gratify all wants, ease all worries, or remove the mark of mortality from our frame. We need some self-control over our wants, some composure in the midst of illness, some courage in the face of dying. No system of itself can bring these virtues to us. We need to bring them to the system so that its benefits may sustain us more fully.

The ancient Romans tended to emphasize the *benefits* of citizenship; the Athenians emphasized its *responsibilities*. The moral and economic success of the reform of our system of health care will require both emphases.

These three foundational judgments about the good of health care and their derivative moral principles do not lie together in easy tranquillity. Tensions will inevitably arise between paying for the fundamental good of health care and providing for other basic goods (and comparatively trivial commodities). The goals of universal and comprehensive coverage will also confront the hurdle of the start-up costs that major changes in both government and business inevitably entail, whatever the eventual economies achieved by reform. Differences will surely develop over priorities in goals, if not over the goals themselves, and about the best mechanisms and institutions by which to reach even agreed-upon goals. President Clinton signaled his own first priority when he lifted his pen during his first major speech on health care and said that he would not sign a bill unless it offered universal coverage. But not long after, he accommodated on the speed with which his plan would move toward that goal (four years) and whether that goal would entail a full 100 percent coverage.

But critics can exaggerate the conflicts between principles and exploit this exaggeration to discredit truly comprehensive reform in favor of very restricted, incremental reform. For example, some members of Congress, fearing that universal coverage would cost too much, have proposed only a few limited steps to increase access to care, such as requiring insurance companies to accept patients with preexisting conditions. This specific reform, they believe, would help us along the way to universal coverage without the burden of mandated premiums, large tax subsidies, or a governmental takeover and bureaucratization of health care.

Such partial reforms, however, can be counterproductive and more costly in the long run. If, for example, one forces insurance companies to accept patients with preexisting conditions ($100,000 cases are not unusual) without other coordinated measures, insurance companies will promptly raise the rates they charge all their customers. In effect, costs will rise and shift from applicants with preexisting conditions to the already insured. Almost as promptly, employers who have previously covered their employees will find reasons to drop this more expensive fringe benefit, and young and healthy employees will not pick up coverage on their own. The net result? In the absence of other coordinated measures, this otherwise very good reform ostensibly aimed at moving the country closer to universal coverage will actually move it farther away from it. We will also exacerbate the current frenzy of cost shifting, which distributes the burdens of paying for health care unfairly and leads to increased costs as the uninsured often delay going to a doctor or a hospital until they require the most expensive services. It is not self-evident that partial reforms best serve the total ecology of a health care system.

The Competing Proposals

Several competing plans have come before Congress and the nation. The pre-1994 conservative plan, eventuating in Sen. Robert Dole's proposal, took the incremental route to reform. Senator Dole hoped to improve access to health care (by means of insurance reforms and monetary assistance to poor families) without making a firm commitment to universal coverage (no mandated premiums for insurance, no additional tax revenues). Senator Dole also relied generally on marketplace competition to control costs rather than budgetary limits of the sort that apply in such fields as education or defense. A drop in the rate of increases in health care costs during the political debates of 1993-94 has strengthened the Republican resolve to reject any government efforts at cost control except as they might apply to Medicare and Medicaid.

Some Democrats viewed the price restraint more skeptically, believing that the threat of reform motivated it. In the past, we have enjoyed pauses in health care inflation only to see prices rise again. Others viewed the drop in the rate of increase in the cost of health care as a more permanent change because they believed that it resulted from the increasing shift of job-insured Americans from a fee-for-service to a much cheaper capitation system of payment under managed care. The latter system strongly motivates doctors to economize on health care, since their income depends upon the difference between the annual fixed payment to providers for care per patient and the cost of services actually rendered. However, the prices charged by HMO's began to rise again in 1995.

The Republican Congress has accented the word *voluntary* as a way of staving off more comprehensive changes. They argue that health care is not so fundamental a good that we must treat it as a basic cost of doing business in America — in the form of compulsory employer contributions to health care coverage. At the same time, other fundamental goods are not so pressing that the government need take steps to bring the cost of health care under control, except for reducing the cost of its own programs for the elderly and the poor and by general reliance on market forces. The accent on the word *voluntary* above other considerations tends to put health care into the basket with other optional commodities.

The word *voluntary* appeals broadly and powerfully to three different constituencies, but it carries a different primary meaning for each group. For patients, *voluntary* means primarily the freedom to choose one's own doctor. For doctors, it means the freedom to practice as they see fit. For employers, however, *voluntary* means freedom from mandated premiums and tax increases; and, for those employers who choose to offer the fringe benefit of health care, it means the freedom to choose the type and terms thereof. Inevitably, however, the conservative's chief hope for cost savings will drastically curtail at least two of these three freedoms. The freedom of employers may be preserved, but the freedom of patients and doctors will diminish. Employers will retain the freedom to reject altogether or bargain on health care coverage for their employees. But the expected reductions in the rate of increase in the cost of health care that they envisage will largely result from shifting their employees from fee-for-service to managed-care programs. That shift will drastically alter and limit the traditional freedoms of doctors and patients. Similarly, the projected savings of $270 billion in the cost of Medicare across the next seven years will derive largely from moving the majority of the elderly from the fee-for-service system that 90 percent of them currently enjoy into managed-care networks. In such provider institutions, doctors largely submit to monitoring by case managers. Such changes may be justified, but not on the grounds that they preserve the freedom each of these constituencies has heretofore enjoyed.

Before the 1994 congressional elections, Senator Kerrey of Nebraska and about 100 other Democrats in the Congress seemed to support the single-payer system of Canada and Great Britain, which relies primarily on the vehicle of a tax-supported, state-administered public insurance plan operating within global budgets. The left wing of the Democratic Party rejected the Clinton proposals for health care reform on the grounds that the Clinton plan for managed competition, all Republican criticism to the contrary, relied much too heavily on marketplace forces to reform the system. The Clinton plan, they predicted, would eventually lead to a handful of huge insurance companies and HMO's running the nation's health care system. The Insurance Council of America, representing the full gamut of insurance companies in the health care business, essentially agreed with the left wing of the Democratic Party and fought the Clinton plan with low-key but effective ads. In general, backers of a single-payer system have typically been charged with proposing socialized medicine and seeking to bring down to the U.S.A. a system that some Canadian doctors and wealthy Canadian patients seek to escape by crossing the border.

President Clinton's original plan sought to achieve universal (95-100 percent) coverage in four years. It also proposed addressing the imbalance between acute and other forms of care, in part through the definition of a comprehensive benefits package and in part through the eventual redeployment of personnel (by adjusting the ratio of specialists to primary care physicians from 7:3 to approximately 1:1 and by increasing the number of nurses in the United States by 700,000). President Clinton proposed paying for health care reform through mandated employer premiums and through taxes, which would continue support for federal programs and subsidize small employers. He sought to control the swiftly rising cost of health care not directly by instituting federal price controls or by the federal micromanagement of individual cases but by marketplace competition among providers over the price and quality of the services they offered to individual subscribers. The buzzword in the Clinton camp was not "managed care" but "managed competition."[1] However, genuine competition in the marketplace requires the existence of (1) at least several different types of provider organizations in a given state to afford the subscriber some choice and (2) suffi-

---

1. The best brief explanation and defense of the Clinton Health Care Proposal for managed competition appeared in Paul Starr's *The Logic of Health Care Reform* (Knoxville: Whittle Communications, 1992).

cient information about outcomes achieved so as to let the subscriber make an informed choice.

The Clinton plan was far less complicated organizationally and far less concentrated federally than critics led the nation to believe. It depended upon three institutions: (1) a National Health Council, a relatively small body to define the basic benefits package that all providers would have to offer as a minimum (this Council would not have micromanaged individual cases as third-party payers currently do); (2) statewide health alliances that would receive mandated premiums and some tax money and act as negotiating agents for citizens, who would choose their own particular plan; and (3) provider organizations that would compete for citizens on the basis of price and quality rather than on the basis of the hitherto important marketing skill of recruiting only those patients who would be unlikely to need expensive services. Provider organizations would not have the power to reject medically at-risk subscribers.

The organizational specifics of the Clinton plan quickly gave way to two differing Democratic plans under the auspices of the House and Senate majority leaders before the 1994 elections. The plan of Rep. Richard Gephardt in the House maintained the employer/employee mandates of the original Clinton plan but dropped the device of the health alliances and tilted somewhat in the direction of the single-payer system by establishing a so-called Medicare C program. This program would have enrolled as many as ninety million Americans by 2004, thus conceivably providing the basis for eventual conversion into a tax-based single-payer system.

Senator Mitchell's plan moved several paces in the opposite direction, toward the more moderate Republicans and conservative Democrats. It aimed for coverage of 95 percent of Americans in six years and would have provided more tax dollars and other incentives to make good on that goal. Mitchell temporarily foreswore mandated premiums, because he wanted to commit the Congress (1) to review further moves if the country failed to reach the targeted goal of 95 percent in six years and (2) to enact mandated premiums should Congress not reach that goal by an alternative route. While more market-oriented than Gephardt's bill, the Mitchell plan did not depend exclusively on the market to keep costs down. Mitchell proposed a 25 percent tax on health insurance plans under which costs grew faster than a prescribed pace.

Why did President Clinton not support a single-payer system from the start, and why in 1994 did he give more support to the Mitchell bill in the Senate than to the more liberal Gephardt bill in the House (which would have created some momentum toward a single-payer system)? The answer lay partly in Clinton's reading of the political situation in the United States. As Paul Starr, a major consultant on managed competition put it, a single-payer system was not in the cards politically in the United States. It was improbable before the 1994 election and impossible afterward. But Clinton's maneuvers also reflected his general philosophy of political change. As a political leader, he resembles more a British than a French gardener. The French produced the garden at Versailles, a triumph of abstract design over the idiosyncrasies of landscape. The British gardener, on the other hand, tends to begin with what's there and trim and prune and enhance it, turning the soil a bit, broadcasting a little seed, and praying for a little sun and rain. To bring the analogy back to Arkansas, Clinton resembles a dirt farmer more than an engineer.

I suspect the President felt that his original proposal (and later that of the Senate) fit the American terrain better than a single-payer system would have. It took advantage of the competitive vitality of the marketplace in this country. While not magical and while not suitable as a sole mechanism for distributing a basic good such as health care, the marketplace can be mobilized and refocused competitively. Hillary Rodham Clinton, especially, emphasized that insurance plans need to compete about the right things — quality and price — not about how to avoid enrolling and paying for people with health problems.

The dramatic shift from a Democratic to a Republican control of both houses of Congress in the 1994 elections shelved all Democratic proposals for major health care reform except for those produced by cooperating Republican and Democratic centrists. But the maneuvering for the presidential nomination in 1996 caused almost all Republican candidates, whatever their prior views, to move to the right. This tactical realignment made it difficult for centrists to secure the active backing of any top party candidate.

The Gingrich wing of the Republican Party identified eliminating the budget deficit and cutting taxes, not reforming the health care system, as its top priorities. Health care reform did not make it into the "Contract with America." Indeed, the Republicans looked to cuts in Medicare funding to achieve projected cumulative savings of $270 billion across the next seven years, in order to generate $240 billion for capital gains and income tax cuts and to cut $30 billion from the budget deficit. To achieve this goal, they hoped to shift many of the elderly, through various financial incentives, from fee-for-service offerings to less expensive managed-care systems. Various strategies have also been suggested to make patients more cost-conscious consumers of health care. Some have suggested giving beneficiaries a one-time opportunity at age sixty-five to set up a medical savings account and enroll in a private plan offering catastrophic insurance coverage as an alternative to any other types of Medicare coverage. Some have proposed increasing Medicare premiums for people with higher incomes and placing a cap on medical malpractice awards. But, other than requiring insurance companies to accept patients with preexistent conditions and assuming in general that managed care will make insurance more affordable, the ruling Republicans have not, at the time of this writing, made any major moves toward providing universal and comprehensive medical coverage.

Some leaders in the Republican Party, including Senators Kassebaum, Gregg, and Gorton, have joined with some Democrats, including Senators Kennedy and Wellstone, to coordinate incremental moves in such a way as to make modest progress toward universal coverage. They recognize that requiring insurance companies to accept patients with preexistent conditions would not of itself, for reasons already given, increase the total number of people covered. Thus centrists on this issue urge providing government subsidies to carriers who have had to accept disproportionate numbers of subscribers in order to keep their insurance rates attractive and competitive.

Fictions and Fears

Just what Washington will decide about the details of health care policy is not yet clear, but it seems certain that the rhetoric of fear and outright fictions will continue to flood the media and swamp the discussion of comprehensive reform. It may be useful, therefore, to attend to some of these persistent fictions and fears, in hopes of returning the debate to the issue of placing our health care system on abiding moral foundations.

1. The Fear of Socialized Medicine

None of the proposals for health care reform in the U.S.A. has recommended socialized medicine — that is, urged that the government own and control the means of production and distribution. Sen. Phil Gramm and others criticized all the Democratic plans as socializing medicine, but the plans endorsed by conservatives and centrists were not categorically different. In fact, the conservatives give a much larger role to the government than their libertarian rhetoric would lead one to believe. They do not propose abolishing Medicare or completely eliminating federal investments in the sort of medical research that helps provide the *armamentarium* of drugs and procedures on which doctors, hospitals, insurance companies, and pharmaceuticals have depended for their livelihoods. They do not propose shutting down veterans' hospitals. They do not demand that the government eliminate support for the training of nurses and doctors in residency programs. They do not want to eliminate the tax deductions for health care insurance given to employers — deductions through which the government influences the sorts of choices available in the marketplace. And some of their suggested reforms would inevitably alter trading in the marketplace in other ways. Requiring insurance companies to accept patients with pre-existing conditions would raise the cost of insurance for those who are already insured. Rising costs would lead businesses to reduce the number of employees that are insured, and the working poor would increasingly end up on some kind of government assistance. In brief, conservatives often inveigh against socialism, but some of their own proposals would also move us farther from a free-market health care system and trigger and expand government interventions in expensive and bureaucratically cumbersome forms.

One cannot accurately characterize the original Clinton plan, whatever its defects, as socialistic. Indeed, as the physician Steven Schroeder, director of the Robert Wood Johnson Foundation, points out, Clinton took "a market-based approach."[2] Under his plan, the federal government, through a National Health Council, would have defined the minimum benefits package available to all citizens, but the actual provision of health care would have come from competing provider organizations. The Clinton plan would further have strengthened one of the key features of any market-based approach: it would have provided consumers with information about cost and quality "hospital by hospital and physician group by physician group on charges, outcomes, mortality rates, and complication rates."[3]

    2. Schroeder, "The Health Care Cost Crisis in America: Too Much of a Good Thing?" *Pharos,* Spring 1994, p. 26.
    3. Schroeder, "The Health Care Cost Crisis in America," p. 26.

Our current system doesn't provide patients with this information, which is crucial for consumers as they attempt to make knowledgeable decisions in a market economy.

Strictly considered, not even proponents of a single-payer system like the "Canadian Plan," which funds medical care through taxes, advocate socialized medicine. Canadian doctors do not work for the government. The government does not control their decisions. No third-party payer in Canada watches over what doctors do, in the fashion of HMOs and Blue Cross/Blue Shield and other insurance companies in America. A single-payer system would reduce the huge bureaucratic redundancies that our current complex system of some 1,500 competing insurance payers supports, and it would drastically reduce the paperwork (and therefore the staffs) that providers, whether physicians or hospitals, must currently maintain. Aware of these facts, a growing minority of U.S. doctors prefers the single-payer Canadian plan to both our current systems of oversight and the Clinton plan.

Discussions of liberty need to distinguish between mercantile liberty and professional liberty. Canadian doctors do not have unlimited mercantile liberty — they cannot charge whatever they want for a given service in the public system. But they do enjoy professional liberty to deliver what they judge necessary for health care without enduring the intrusion of the sort of third-party and case managers in the provider organization that currently beset professional practice in this country.

2. The Fear of Bureaucratization

Doctors and hospital administrators especially fear the growth of bureaucracy, because the current system already groans under the weight of it. However, we are wrong if we suppose that only government agencies are bureaucratic. As one executive in the private sector mordantly observed, bureaucrats work for insurance companies as well as for the government. Bureaucracies grow, public and private, partly because people and organizations become suspicious of the discretionary exercise of power. To block the abuse or misuse of power, they seek to standardize procedures and develop elaborate mechanisms for oversight to ensure that people conform to those procedures. Unchecked, these mechanisms for oversight will eventually immobilize the participants. Medical practitioners are kept so busy conforming to procedures (and proving that they are conforming) that they have less time to heal. Our shorthand name for this clogging of the system is "paperwork" — the bane of doctors, hospital administrators, and patients alike.

In our current system, the bureaucratic blight is serious for two reasons. First, as we have already noted, over 1,500 insurance companies compete for the health care dollar, generating huge redundancies in administrative and advertising costs (as much as 40 percent of the cost of insurance for a small employer can go to administration). The bureaucratic blight also imposes enormous billing costs on hospitals and doctors. Second, the current American system has institutionalized micromanaging at a distance. Oversight has run amok. Payers — such as the government and Blue Cross/Blue Shield and other insurance companies — now insist on signing off on individual procedures for individual patients. The original Clinton plan tried to tackle this problem of metastasizing bureaucracy by specifying that neither the federal government (through its National Health Council) nor the health alliances at the state level would set up bureaucracies for micromanaging medical decisions. The detailed decisions in individual cases would be left in the hands of the provider organization, in which, presumably, professionals and patients would have a direct say according to established procedures of informed consent. The scheme was not perfect, since in general professionals (doctors, teachers, lawyers) have not yet satisfactorily worked out how they can offer professional advice and influence in the setting of large-scale provider bureaucracies (hospitals, universities, law firms). Still, the proposal sought to reduce the kind of bureaucratic oversight at a distance that has particularly vexed practitioners today, whether they deal with the government or insurance companies.

3. The Fear of Rationing

Opponents charge that some variant of the Clinton plan or the single-payer system will impose rationing of health care on the nation. Meanwhile, proponents of reform have avoided the dread "R" word in favor of the less radioactive phrase "setting priorities."

In fact, we already ration care — and badly — when we fail to provide coverage for one out of seven Americans and when we lavish money on acute care in the last two to six months of life, oftentimes prolonging the ordeal of dying while neglecting the merciful sorts of care that would ease dying. All plans that have come before Congress entail rationing, either by maintaining the current basic distributions of money or by setting different priorities. The advocates of reform might be better off facing the issue of rationing head-on instead of avoiding the term. We already do it. We cannot escape it. We ought to do it better.

Daniel Callahan, perhaps more than any other writer, has taken an unblinking look at the issue of rationing health care. In a series of three books, he has argued that we underestimate the long-range economic problem if we think we will contain rising costs by cutting out inefficiencies, waste, and administrative redundancies, by capping malpractice awards, or by instituting the devices of advance directives or durable powers of attorney.[4] Neither will we substan-

4. See Callahan, *Setting Limits: Medical Goals in an Aging Society* (New York: Simon & Schuster, 1987); *What Kind of Life? The Limits of Medical Progress* (New York: Simon & Schuster, 1990); and *The Troubled Dream of Life: Living with Mortality* (New York: Simon & Schuster, 1993).

tially reduce the pressures on the delivery system by distinguishing needs from wants and beneficial from futile treatments. Rather, we will have to distinguish between needs and needs and between benefits and benefits. Such hard choices cut to the bone of the problem of rationing. While a fundamental good, health care is not the only fundamental good. Callahan criticizes a society in which the hospital is usually the best equipped and the high school the worst equipped public building in the city. None of the health care proposals currently before the nation has addressed these issues in rationing which will certainly be our portion in the twenty-first century.

4. The Fear That Universal Coverage Would Require Workers to Foot the Bill for the Idle

Some have opposed universal medical coverage on the grounds that it would disproportionately penalize working people by forcing them to pay for the coverage of people who do not work. The fact of the matter, however, is that some 84 percent of Americans who lack insurance coverage do work. They are the working poor — many of them in low-paying service jobs at discount stores, fast food chains, gas stations, convenience stores, and the like. Most plans propose providing some assistance to workers. The Dole plan called for government subsidies of this sort, although they declined precipitously as income rose. An average health care premium costs a family of four about $6,800 per year. Under the Dole plan, such a family, working at the poverty level of $14,800 (in 1994), would have received a 100 percent subsidy, but the subsidy would have phased out when family income reached 1.5 times the poverty level — $22,200. Thus, of the first $7,400 that the family had earned above the poverty level (since employers need not have contributed to their insurance), some $6,800 would have gone to buy medical insurance. That would have been an effective marginal tax rate of ninety cents on the dollar. In this fashion, the Dole proposal defied the traditional capitalist assumption about the psychology of the marketplace — namely, that self-interest and profit supply its driving force. Conservatives have opposed significantly smaller tax increases on the grounds that they blunt incentives to work hard. For example, over the years, they worked to reduce the marginal tax rates on the wealthy from the 70 percent to the low 30 percent range, and some have argued for a flat tax as low as 15 percent. The scheme of steeply reducing subsidies for medical insurance seems to assume that only the wealthy, not the poor, need the motive of self-interest to work.

5. The Fear That Employer Mandates Will Hurt Businesses and Cost Jobs

Many argue that any plan that places an additional burden on employers to provide health care benefits to their employees would have a dire effect on business generally, especially small businesses and those that principally employ people in part-time and minimum-wage positions. This prediction flies in the face of the only experience we have had in the United States with mandated employer contributions: Hawaii. That state has had a lower rate of unemployment, a better record of general health, and a much lower cost of supplementary health insurance than other states. The burden of proof rests on critics to show why their gloomy predictions will come true this time around on health care legislation. Meanwhile, we face the irony that such companies as McDonald's and Pizza Hut provide health care coverage to their service employees in Germany and Japan but deny coverage to comparable workers in the U.S.A.

The Pain of Change

The track record of Hawaii and all major industrial countries suggests that universal and comprehensive coverage, whether supported through taxes or mandated premiums, would keep costs under control better than minor incrementalist reforms of our current system. However, dislocations in employment would occur. Many bureaucratic jobs in the 1,500 insurance companies doing business in health care would disappear, for example. (Of course, many such jobs are already disappearing under the steam of the current system, as managed care through marketplace operations seems to be replacing fee-for-service medicine. But Americans seem to be more tolerant of layoffs caused by the marketplace than those caused by the government. That tolerance is part of the magic of the marketplace.) Some doctors would need to retool as they shifted to a more general practice. On the other hand, though, significant health care reform would also create new jobs. We would need some 700,000 more nurses if we shifted to more comprehensive care. It has been estimated that on the whole the total layoffs and new jobs would balance out. Still, some segments of the workforce would be traumatized. Major changes would entail start-up costs before long-term savings kicked in, and they would impose hikes in the cost of doing business for many firms whose employees have been tempted or coerced to freeload under the current system.

Thus advocates of major reforms have had to devise various schemes for phasing in mandated premiums and/or changes in tax law should the country move toward universal and comprehensive coverage. Three different versions of "phasing in" mandated premiums surfaced before the 1994 elections. The first called for instituting mandated premiums immediately but providing subsidies to small businesses and the working poor to ease the transition. The second, Senator Mitchell's so-called "hard trigger" plan, called for imposing mandated premiums automatically if a target of 95 percent insured were not reached voluntarily in six years and if Congress had provided no other plan to reach universal coverage. The third, "soft trigger" plan merely called on Congress to reconsider the issue at a later date if the country fell short of the target. In effect, it punted the issue of universal coverage into the next millennium and encouraged employers and employees, for some of the reasons already cited, to drop or reduce insurance coverage in the interim.

What about the political chances of passing major new health care legislation in this millennium? Will we be willing to make significant changes in the foreseeable future? My tragic law of politics goes as follows: we see a problem and agree to solve it only after the solution is beyond reach. We could have reformed the health care system much more easily when Harry Truman said we needed to do it in 1948, when health care costs were 4.5 percent of the GNP. That amount was significant but modest compared with our health care costs today, which have risen past 14 percent of a comparable measure of the nation's economy. Eleven million people now have jobs in the industry, some of them ready to attack any changes that might affect their interests. Gridlocks in government usually reflect gridlocks of various kinds in society at large. Undoubtedly, public backing for major health care reform also depends in part on the state of the economy. The economy must not be so bad that the country feels it cannot afford the start-up costs of reform but not so good that currently insured workers are unconcerned about losing their jobs or their health care coverage.

However, I am not unrelievedly pessimistic. President Clinton at least managed to put the problem on the national agenda if not in the Contract with America, and 60 percent of the voters have at one time or another said they would consider some rise in taxes in order to provide universal coverage. Still, politics, as Max Weber once put it, is, at best, slow boring through hard wood. Political solutions are *possible* but *difficult* — a good deal more difficult than my fellow Texan Ross "Just Lift up the Hood and Fix It" Perot is willing to admit.

To achieve major reform, we cannot treat health care simply as a partisan or an interest-group issue. We will need to return to our foundations as a people. Our founders assumed that if a nation could create a common good, it should make that good common. We can now deliver health care to all our people, and this good will help secure and enhance the life, liberty, and welfare that is our nation's promise to its citizens. It is time to reconfirm that promise to one another. Such a renewal of a covenant seems difficult, coming, as it does, so late in the day and with well-established interests already in the field. It will surely require a broad appeal to self-interest. But it will also need to appeal to what Lincoln called "the better angels of our nature," those angels that Tocqueville must have discerned when he wrote that a "covenant exists . . . between all the citizens of a democracy when they all feel themselves subject to the same weakness and the same dangers; their interests as well as their compassion makes it a rule with them to lend one another assistance when required."

*　　*　　*

A Theological Postscript

I want to close this chapter and the book with a Christian justification for health care reform. I decided not to begin the chapter with the Christian warrants for reform on the grounds that this placement might mislead. It might bind together too deductively Christian theological affirmations with the three "foundations" I outlined, a tightening that might lead to several errors. For one thing, it might leave too little room for good-faith differences among Christians — if not on foundations and derivative principles, certainly on their relative weight. This loss of reflective space might, in turn, leave too little room for subsequent theological criticism of a particular design and its institutional realization. It might also imply that only Christians could arrive at these foundations, a restriction difficult to justify. One need not hold to the Christian faith in order to affirm that health care is a fundamental and public good among other such goods.

At the same time, I believed that this chapter required reflection at some point on the theological tradition as it bears on the question of health care reform. Otherwise, I would, by implication, yield to those secularists and religionists who would distance religion from politics to the enfeeblement of the first and the impoverishment of both.

The secular objections to religious involvement in health care reform are familiar enough. Some secular participants in the debate over health care reform would like to keep religious language out of the discussion altogether. They appeal to the principle of the separation of church and state or fear the divisiveness of religious language in the political arena.

Both secular reasons for removing religious language from the public arena are too indiscriminate. The First Amendment clearly prohibits the enactment of laws for purely religious *purposes,* such as the establishment or advancement of a particular religious tradition, but it hardly intends to deny to citizens religious *motives* and *reasons* for believing and acting and voting as they do on matters of public purpose and the common good. Nor does it deny them the right to explain these motives and reasons to others. The First Amendment does not confine religious liberty purely to the private sphere. This restriction would flagrantly overlook the careful location of religious liberty in the Amendment, among the freedoms of speech, assembly, and the press. These four liberties belong together in that they are not purely private liberties. Each supplies the means by which people assemble together through the spoken and written word to deliberate and reach their judgments on matters of great moment. As William Lee Miller has observed in *The First Liberty,* the founders clustered the four liberties in the First Amendment in order to undergird the deliberative process in a republic.[5] They wanted to ensure the health and vigor of public discussion and debate about questions of the common good. To protect the deliberative process, the Amendment forbids any legislative, executive, or judicial action that would establish a particular religious tradition over others or over those citizens who reject religious belief. But the Amendment does not single out religious communities and deny them the right to participate in deliberations about the common good that the other liberties therein sited so obviously enable.

Others fear that religious language is inherently divisive and therefore unsuitable for discourse about common political purposes, that it too quickly excludes those who are not in the know. But what are we to make, then, of Lincoln's appeal to religious language in helping the nation recover its badly shattered unity toward the end of the Civil War? In Lincoln's time and in our own, we misread the politics of the nation if we assume that we are indeterminately a public, religious or secular. The health of the nation depends upon our recognizing that, in forging national policies, we must appeal to publics within a public — among them, religious publics with their own particular memories, beliefs, and motives for action that bear on questions of public purpose.

Two forms of the Christian tradition itself generate a still further reluctance to enter into debate on such public issues as health care reform. Sectarians tend to despair of the general social and political order altogether and would restrict the moral mandates of the faith to the formation of a distinctive Christian culture cut off from its

5. Miller, "On the Underpinnings of Republicanism," in *The First Liberty: Religion and the American Republic* (New York: Alfred A. Knopf, 1986), pp. 343-53.

surroundings. They renounce efforts to engage the society at large in the question of the bettering of its institutional forms, and they despair of coalitions between religious communities and other publics. Their dismissal reminds me of the comment of the nineteenth-century bishop of Chicester whose amiable stroll down the street with a friend was interrupted by two men arguing with one another from open windows on opposite sides of the road. Those men will never agree, the bishop said; they are arguing from opposite premises.

Sectarians believe that the church and other communities in the society at large cannot work for common ends without compromising the purity of the church's life and message. In effect, they can imagine only two ways in which the church might relate to the social and political order: either by a Constantinian domination of the world, with all the attendant dangers of corrupting the church's substance, or by a strict separation from the world for the sake of the church's pure witness to a kingdom not of this earth. The sectarian worries that, rather than the yeast leavening the loaf, the loaf will compromise the yeast.

The second Christian reticence springs not from sectarian denial of the world but from a Lutheran modesty about the church's role in the political order. Gilbert Meilaender in *Faith and Faithfulness* offers an apt contemporary statement of this position. He limits the church's social and political action to interventions of two sorts: (1) occasional negative, prophetic judgments against the political order for egregious wrongs (such as the Nazi genocide policies) and (2) small-scale corporal works of mercy that the Church undertakes directly (such as those enunciated in Isa. 61:1-2 and 58:6, which Jesus cites at the beginning of his ministry, or those tests of righteousness that he sets forth in his parable on the last judgment, Matt. 25). Beyond that, says Meilaender, the church should keep its voice out of politics. This Lutheran approach, while respecting the church's distinctive role, insufficiently honors, in my judgment, the degree to which the gospel itself, while not supplying us with templates for political institutions, does furnish us narratively with standards by which our imperfect work in the arena of politics may be measured.

Access to the Healing Pool

Scripture does not use the language of the modern debate. The narratives of the New Testament in Koine Greek are mercifully free of the Latinate tags *universal, comprehensive,* and the like. But neither do such words force the narratives.

A story in the Gospel of John provides a parable for a health care system that gives access to all:

Now in Jerusalem by the Sheep Gate there is a pool, called in Hebrew Beth-zatha, which has five porticos. In these lay many invalids — blind, lame, and paralyzed. One man was there who had been ill for thirty-eight years. When Jesus saw him lying and knew that he had been there a long time, he said to him, "Do you want to be made well?" The sick man answered him, "Sir, I have no one to put me into the pool when the water is stirred up; and while I am making my way, someone else steps ahead of me. Jesus said to him, "Stand up, take your mat and walk." At once the man was made well and he took up his mat and began to walk. (5:2-9)

Through many such stories, the gospels emphasize the outreach and the scope of Jesus' ministry as a healer. He heals the outsiders, those who don't have access to the good of healing, and his healing takes diverse forms depending upon need. He cleanses lepers, he breaks the hold of demonic and destructive powers that assault the afflicted, and he restores still others to bodily integrity as he empowers them to see, hear, and walk.

These stories feature the Savior as the healer of illness and also serve as signs of the larger work of redemption accomplished through his coming and the inauguration of God's reign. Jesus' healing miracles are not haphazard. They fall into three types: those that cleanse, those that liberate from demonic and destructive power, and those that restore the sufferer to bodily integrity and health. Together, these different types of healing serve as signs of the cleansing, liberating, and restorative work that God accomplishes through Jesus' ministry, death, and resurrection.[6]

Still, while the miracles point beyond the healing episodes to the larger saving work of God, they also say something directly and immediately about the human good of health and the work of healing. Health is a fundamental, not a trivial, good. Men and women instinctively, urgently, and passionately seek it out. They thirst for healing as for water. Thus the place of healing, like an oasis in the desert, quickly becomes a public place. Healing is a public good, and only too quickly a scarce public good. But the Savior-healer swiftly reaches out to those who have no access to the good and extends it to them — the resourceless, the needy, those with no money to turn the stile, no insurance card to flash their way into the hospital, no motorized wheelchair to bring them up to the edge of the healing waters. Were health and healing trivial goods, exclusion would not matter. But healing is a fundamental good, and therefore it should reach everybody: all should have access to the healing pool. Health care coverage should be universal.

The diversity of Jesus' miracles also recognizes that healing itself

6. The healing miracles of cleansing serve as signs of God's forgiving love (justifying grace); the miracles of liberation and restoration point to God's empowering love (sanctifying grace). The tradition also recognized two aspects to sanctifying or empowering grace: the negative task of liberation from demonic power and the positive task of restoration to our full, intended powers. Together, these three aspects of grace reflect the saving work of Christ as summarized in the doctrine of the atonement: the forensic work of forgiveness, the military work of victory over destructive power, and the subjective work of restoration to our intended powers.

is diverse. The needs of the sick vary, and therefore health care itself must be diverse — that is, comprehensive. Jesus does not heal the lame at the expense of the halt and the blind, or the deaf at the expense of the scurvied and the tormented. Indeed, to be universal, health care must also be comprehensive. To reach all those in need, it must address the full range of needs.

The importance of the notion of universality and the intimate connection between universality and comprehensiveness show up in the later doctrine of the catholicity of the church. The ancient credal affirmation of the church as catholic traces back to Scripture. The New Testament takes care to treat Jesus' works of healing as signs. They do not simply serve as a basket of goods that temporarily meet needs; they point beyond themselves to a supreme good, which Jesus himself inaugurates and incarnates. Moreover, the church believed that this supreme good, the self-expending love of God, must reach everybody. This belief informed that strangely urgent missionary impulse that has characterized Christianity from the beginning. "Go into all the nations and baptize them. . . ." Later in history, this missionary impulse to spread rather than hoard the supreme good strayed from the exuberant love that originally propelled it. The missionary impulse distorted into the urge to conquer, to rule, to coerce, and to exploit. But the original impulse arose from a sense that the supreme good, the ultimate good, belongs to no one; it should divide no one from others; it should not divide humankind into the haves and the have-nots. Indeed, a reluctance to share this supreme good would surely betray a want of love.

Thus the early church used the word *catholicity* to describe one of its primary marks apart from which the church defected from its mission.[7] Early Christians viewed the church as universal and seized

7. For a discussion of catholicity and its implications for the professions, see William F. May, *The Physician's Covenant* (Louisville: Westminster/John Knox Press, 1983).

upon the image of the ark to describe its universal mission. They wrote of an "ark of salvation" open to all creatures, familiar and strange, beautiful and grotesque, irrespective of shape, color, size, gender, wealth, or age. Societies may organize themselves into the rich and poor, the haves and have-nots, but the church, as bearer of the supreme good, must, at least in principle, make the word and sacraments available to all who confess their need.

Derivatively and analogously, fundamental goods such as health care — goods less than supreme but still fundamental to human life and flourishing — should reach all in need. The services of physicians and others in the helping professions should extend beyond the parochial, restricting, and excluding boundaries that ordinary life establishes. These life- and health-serving goods should extend to the stranger and the needy. A profession becomes corrupted if it falls captive to the interests of a particular class. Physicians and nurses (and the society that arranges for their services) lose much that belongs to their moral substance if they merely hire out in contracts to serve a single class — if they lose the mark, as it were, of catholicity.

Further, the theologians eventually distinguished between two dimensions of the church's catholicity: external and internal. External catholicity refers to the church's mission to reach the whole of humankind, what we have already identified as the church's universality. Its internal catholicity refers to the church's obligation to meet the needs of the whole person, body and soul. (The Catholic theologian Karl Adam, for example, argued that an overly intellectual Protestantism emphasized the preaching of the Word at the expense of other ingredients in worship that address the senses of sight, sound, and smell.)[8]

Correspondingly, in distributing the fundamental good of health care, we must not only meet the needs of the whole public (the

8. See chapter 9 of Adam's *Spirit of Catholicism* (New York: Image Books, 1954).

standard of universality) but also address the whole needs of the public (the standard of comprehensiveness). If the first obligation requires that the health care system reaches everybody, the second requires the development of the full manifold of services needed — that is, preventive, rehabilitative, long-term, and terminal care as well as acute care and treatment for mental as well as physical illness. These standards are distinct but related. When a profession or a system fails to develop a full range of services, it also fails to reach the entire population in need.

The Scripture narratives make a second point about healing with implications for a health care system. While healing is a fundamental good, it is not the only fundamental good, nor does it rank with the supreme good to which the acts of healing point. At the beginning of his ministry, Jesus reads a passage from Isaiah:

> The Spirit of the Lord is upon me,
> Because he has anointed me to bring good news to the poor.
> He has sent me to proclaim release to the captives
> And recovery of sight to the blind,
> To let the oppressed go free,
> To proclaim the year of the Lord's favor.

This passage points to a series of other fundamental goods upon which the full flourishing of a community and its members depends: healing, but also food, clothing, and shelter for the poor and justice for captives and the oppressed.

Further, these several goods are but the signs of a supreme good at hand. Health and healing are goods that derive from God. They signify the imminent work of God, but they are not themselves God. Their status has implications for piety and policy. The goodness of healing authorizes us to pray for it and commit resources to it. But healing is not the sole good or even the chief good, and therefore we cannot pray for it — or fund it — as though health and health care are all that matter. We are authorized to pray for life and healing, but not too desperately. Jesus prayed, "Father, let this cup pass from me; nevertheless, not my will but thine be done."

This scriptural placement of healing in the setting of other goods suggests that health care ought not to crowd out budgetary support for other fundamental goods in the total economy of a society. The rapidly increasing cost of health care since World War II in the U.S.A. makes it clear that the economic question of cost effectiveness is a moral question of properly honoring and balancing priorities; and in the background of the economic and moral questions lies the religious question of stewardship. How do we distribute the fundamental good of health care universally and comprehensively and yet prudently and efficiently enough so as to honor our responsibilities to other goods? Religiously considered, policy makers, providers, and recipients of health care, in differing ways, are stewards of goods received not wholly their own.

Scripture does not provide us with a scheme or design for producing, balancing, and distributing basic goods, but it strikes the great themes that we need to work through in our common life. In my judgment, we wrongly diminish the scope of these scriptural themes if we restrict the church's role and voice to delivering corporal works of mercy and withdraw altogether from the arena of politics, as though God's grace penetrates only the sphere of the personal and the intimate. The logic of God's corporal works of mercy requires efforts at institutional reform. Nurturing institutions — even of the tax-supported variety — may sometimes intimate and foreshadow the kingdom of God.

Index

137